Bob Fitrakis

The Fitrakis Files: Spooks, Nukes & Nazis

Edited by Brian Lindamood

A Columbus Institute for
Contemporary Journalism Book

Published by Columbus Alive Publishing

This book is dedicated to Suzanne Patzer,
my co-conspirator.

Acknowledgements

This collection is largely investigative journalism. As a political scientist, I was never formally trained in this area. Thus, I owe a huge debt to my mentor, Martin Yant, who taught me how the game is played. I regard Marty as the best investigative reporter in Ohio and one of the best in the nation. In a series of books that include *Tin Star Tyrants*, *Rotten to the Core* and *Desert Mirage*, he's uncovered mounds of corruption and moved our system more towards justice. (Marty also originally suggested that I look into Battelle's anthrax research, which became the report on page 23 of this collection.)

Columbus Free Press Editor Duane Jager recruited me as a news writer through sheer persistence, and later talked me into publishing the *Free Press*, as he moved on to organizing in Appalachia.

The late sheriff of Franklin County, Earl Smith, who used to laugh and say, "Sure I'm corrupt, but I'm the least corrupt guy in the county," proved an invaluable source on CIA activity in Franklin County. As a former member of Governor James Rhodes' crime task force, he provided useful insights on organized crime in Ohio and supplied easily verifiable information and interesting documents.

More important, Smith and his family were a pleasure to be around and I always found him to be straightforward and truthful, no matter how hard the questions. The old sheriff also intervened when my life was being threatened. Smith's advice was always thoughtful, whether it was how to get people to talk or understanding the history of politics in Franklin County.

James McNamara and the Anti-Racist Action activists were generous in sharing their own investigative reports on white supremacists. I was privileged to have marched and been Maced with them (page 179). ARA taught me the reality of police brutality, albeit in a painful way.

Tim Wagner suggested the original *Free Press* articles on Battelle (page 89) and was instrumental in providing information on that bizarre institute.

I thank the courageous and resilient parents in Marion, Ohio, who refused to accept the "official explanation" when their children were being poisoned by radioactive and toxic waste (page 107). I was little more than a conduit for the information they gathered.

I'd be remiss if I didn't thank all the reliable sources who prefer to remain unnamed—you know who you are. And anyone who reads this book will understand why they wish to remain anonymous.

Jamie Pietras co-wrote "Uncovering River Valley Schools' Atomic Secrets" (page 110) with me. That story was awarded first place by the Ohio Society of Professional Journalists for environmental reporting. It's no coincidence that I wrote another article with Jamie the next year that won another first-place award for best criminal justice reporting. I have no doubt in the long run that Jamie will prove to be a more notable reporter than me.

David Schalliol undertook the tedious task of assembling all my *Columbus Alive* writings to be used in this book, and I thank him.

The photo of a Southern Air Transport cargo jet parked on the tarmac at Rickenbacker International Airport (page 5) was taken by Brian Lindamood. The aerial photo of the U.S. Army's Marion Engineer Depot (page 87) was taken by the government in 1960; it was provided to us by Marion activist Mike Griffith (the mysterious triangle of disturbed soil in the center of the picture is approximately where the River Valley Schools are now situated). Chris Ryan took the photo of the Ku Klux Klan march (page 147) for the *Free Press*. Holly Vaske designed the cover of this book. Rhonda Files re-typed the older *Free Press* articles, and Alex Mitchell kept me from being beaten at a Klan rally. Thanks.

Finally, I want to acknowledge my two editors, Brian Lindamood and Suzanne Patzer. As an investigative reporter I have an inherent distrust of editors, yet you can trust Brian with your copy. Everything Brian's ever touched, he's noticeably improved. And he never cuts the really good stuff. He was the driving force behind this volume.

My partner and co-conspirator Suzanne Patzer had to endure frantic late-night dictation during many of these stories. Although not officially my editor, she never yielded in her insistence that I write in a style that people could actually understand. The clarity in these writings is the result of her efforts; any confusion is solely my responsibility.

Suzanne and I continue our collaboration with the *Free Press*, published by the nonprofit Columbus Institute for Contemporary Journalism, the recipient of half the profits from this book. If you wish to investigate, you can start at www.freepress.org.

Contents

SPOOKS

NUKES

NAZIS

Introduction

In the nearly five years I edited Bob Fitrakis' columns and investigative reports for *Columbus Alive*, I received complaints about him from just about everyone. Conservatives point to Bob as the embodiment of the liberal media, but liberals throw a fit when he doesn't parrot what they perceive to be "correct" progressive arguments. Republicans have complained that he's a partisan Democrat, while at least one Democrat has complained that he's some kind of secret agent working for the Republicans—I swear I'm not making this up—who, I guess, serves his conservative masters by making liberals look bad from the inside.

Bob Fitrakis serves no one, of course, and he certainly doesn't toe anyone's party line. He has a mind of his own, which has frustrated critics and even a lot of his fans—from all points on the ideological spectrum—who've tried to pigeonhole him.

But there's one thing with which Fitrakis' critics have never been able to argue: The facts. He may be a pain in the ass, but he's a pain in the ass armed with unassailable evidence, and that's what good investigative reporting is all about.

Fitrakis is a classic muckraker, in the great tradition of I.F. Stone and George Seldes. He doesn't just write about issues or news topics, he sinks his teeth into them, mixing solid evidence and thorough research with an even stronger point of view, all guided by a moral compass that points directly to populism, not partisanship.

One of the benefits of this fierce independence is not only that Fitrakis' readers know they can trust him, potential sources do as well. This is a big part of investigative reporting—many of the most important stories start with an anonymous or confidential tip or leaked document. It's also why Fitrakis' home phone number is listed in the phone book, despite his high profile and no lack of potential harassers. You get the best tips, he told me, when sources know they can drop a dime at midnight, away from the glare of office lights (or sunlight), and without risking being identified.

Another of Fitrakis' skills that's left me awestruck over the years is his ability to wade through reams of government documents, quickly digesting the most relevant details and even, sometimes, being able to identify and walk away with the fabled smoking gun.

A lot of the stories in this book were based on publicly available documents and reports (like the international antics of BCCI, or the Army's past activities at the site of the Marion public schools), but it took someone with Fitrakis' analytical abilities to sort through the disjointed mountain of information and piece it together in a way that makes sense for readers. Some of the most damning evidence is buried in plain sight. You just have to know where to look for it—and you have to know what it is when you see it.

For instance, when we were looking into the CIA's ties to Southern Air Transport, a cargo airline that was then based in Columbus, our public records request to the port authority here was answered with, basically, "There's too much stuff to photocopy, come look for yourself."

So we did. Fitrakis and I spent most of one day in a windowless, 10-by-10 storage room at Rickenbacker airport; book shelves lined one wall, file cabinets covered another, with more folders and papers piled on top of the cabinets. Most of it didn't concern SAT, of course, but that was the point: Somewhere in there, buried among thousands of papers and reports, were the few documents Fitrakis was looking for (which, in the end, proved what he had suspected).

I've never known Fitrakis to be wrong, even if it takes him years to be proved right (or, at least, years for the mainstream media to acknowledge that he was right). He exposed Republican politicians' ties to racist and white supremacist organizations before it was fashionable to admit to the GOP's "past" associations with the states' rights South. Fitrakis singled out now-disgraced Senator Trent Lott for his racist ties—back in 1999.

In 1997, Fitrakis wrote about Ohio State Representative William G. Batchelder's reported membership in the little-known and highly secretive far-right Council for National Policy, whose members included "a former Ku Klux Klan leader and others who champion segregationist policies." Interestingly, just this month Governor Bob Taft floated Batchelder's name as a possibility to fill a vacancy on the Ohio Supreme Court. A Taft spokesperson said Batchelder has a "sterling reputation." Maybe we should send the governor a copy of this book.

In 1999, Fitrakis wrote about Echelon, the U.S. National Security Agency's top-secret program to eavesdrop on the world's digital communications. This was long before the government openly acknowledged that it doesn't care much for Americans' supposed civil liberties or right to privacy. (Of course, as it turns out, Echelon wasn't quite as effective as the intelligence community would have hoped anyway.)

Also back in 1999, Fitrakis started reporting on the Bush family's ties to the Bank of Credit and Commerce International, a Pakistani bank whose shadowy spider web of alleged activities included drug-money laundering, arms sales to Iraq and Iran and support of Afghanistan's Mujahedin (and you know how U.S. support for the Mujahedin turned out).

And Fitrakis tried to warn Columbus residents about possible research activities at the mysterious Battelle Memorial Institute, years before anyone worried that the United States' chemical, biological and nuclear weapons experiments could come back to haunt us in a post-September 11 world.

You can imagine the sort of warm response we get from the subjects of these stories. And let's not forget about the CIA, U.S. military, officials at all levels of government, Reverend Sun Myung Moon, the Klan and the rest of the white supremacist community, just to name a few of Fitrakis' closest friends. But he's never shirked from criticism—and he's never backed off—no matter how powerful (or threatening) are the people trying to get him to back off.

It's a testament to Bob Fitrakis' skill as a journalist that he's managed to anger just about everyone at one time or another. Good investigative reporters don't leave anyone happy.

Except for their readers, that is.

Brian Lindamood
January 2003

Dissent: Now More Than Ever

Thirty years ago this month the *Columbus Free Press* ran an ad for the first Community Festival. The journal is two years older than the festival, but a product of the same cultural and political rebellion against the war in Vietnam and the "plastic" suburban culture of the post-WW II era.

It's also the 30th anniversary of the Watergate break-in. The bungled burglary revealed a secret world of shadowy former CIA agents bugging the headquarters of the Democratic Party and working fulltime on dirty tricks to rig the 1972 election. President Nixon's resignation in 1974 left many progressives with false hope of a better America.

The editorial staff of the *Columbus Free Press* was jailed 30 years ago—on May 18, 1972. They were arrested by the notorious Columbus police "Red Squad." Margaret Sarber, John Miernik, Steve Abbott and Colin Neiberger were held as enemies of the state on bail as high as $150,000. Back then, there was a real clash of cultures: a peace-oriented social justice culture versus a violent military industrial complex.

Today, sadly, there's little clash. The Bush administration has taken advantage of the 9/11 tragedy, along with his Christian Coalition Attorney General John Ashcroft, to systematically repeal, suspend and roll back civil liberties. The FBI is authorized to search homes without warrants and without probable cause. The CIA is unleashed to get "down in the mud" with its drug-running allies and create its own paramilitary unit.

The massive documented failures of the national security apparatus—from the National Security Agency to the CIA to the FBI—which allowed terrorists to train at U.S. flight schools and go their way unmolested, are rewarded with more and more power for these agencies and bureaus.

The happy-face fascism of our New England preppie turned faux Texan is routinely accepted by a compliant populace. The NSA's Echelon, the FBI's Carnivore and Magic Lantern are used to create an Orwellian spy apparatus for Big Brother with a Texas drawl.

And nobody's supposed to state the obvious. The CIA, the Saudis and the Pakistani Inter-Service Intelligence Agency are responsible for the so-called Islamic fundamentalist terrorism.

One more time, the evil one, Zbigniew Brzezinski, created the policy to actively support the Afghan Mujahedin in April 1979 (he bragged about it in his interview in *Le Nouvel Observateur* in January 1998). In May 1979, John J. Reagan, the CIA's Islamabad station chief, met with the Afghan resistance leaders and set up the weapons pipeline to topple the pro-Soviet government of Afghanistan. President Carter signed the first secret directive granting aid to the Islamic fundamentalists in July 1979.

The rest is history. The Soviets invaded Afghanistan. At the end of the year the opium-enriched Bank of Credit and Commerce International was funding a war to drive the Soviets out.

Missing in President Bush's recent OSU commencement speech, where he propagandized that the U.S. was the greatest force for good in the world, is the real history surrounding

Afghanistan and the 9/11 attacks. The U.S. and their Saudi and Pakistani allies recruited the most religiously radical and fanatical Islamic extremists to counter the Soviet forces. Literally, the U.S. spent billions to flood Afghanistan with weapons, including Stinger missiles. The fanatics were trained in Pakistani camps supported by the CIA and the Saudis.

When the Soviets were driven out in 1989, what remained in Afghanistan was a bizarre coalition led by Osama bin Laden, a sophisticated, well-educated multi-millionaire with high-level connections to the Saudi royal family, the CIA and the Bush family, in partnership with the rural reactionary Taliban.

The U.S. military-industrial complex created the terrorists and now the Bush administration is demanding that we sacrifice our constitutional rights in an endless war against his and his daddy's former allies and close family friends.

Who's benefiting from the 9/11 terrorist attacks? The 1.5 billion Muslims who are potential targets? The thousands of innocent civilians slaughtered in Afghanistan? The Palestinians brutally attacked by General Sharon under the guise of supporting Bush's war on terrorism? Or the military-industrial complex and the U.S. national security bureaucracy?

Bush's popularity now has an unprecedented high rating, the CIA has a blank check and military spending is at the highest levels in recorded history. In the words of President Eisenhower: "Beware the military-industrial complex."

In the words of the *Free Press*: "Beware the national security state." Dissent—now, more than ever.

Columbus Free Press
July 17, 2002

SPOOKS

What Is Echelon?

Big Brother may not be watching us here in the U.S. but he sure as hell is listening. That's why the American Civil Liberties Union's November 1999 announcement that they've launched a website designed to monitor and investigate a global electronic surveillance system known by the code name "Echelon" is so important.

The ACLU website, echelonwatch.org, promotes public discussion of the potential threat Echelon poses to all our civil liberties. It also provides an extensive collection of research documents on Echelon. Investigative journalists ferreted out bits and pieces of the Echelon puzzle over many years. Last year, the existence of Echelon became an international issue when the European Parliament received two detailed reports on its operations and the Australian government confirmed its participation in the Echelon project.

Echelon is an attempt to capture all satellite, microwave, cellular and fiber-optic communications worldwide, including communications to and from the United States. U.S. National Security Agency (NSA) computers then use sophisticated filtering technology to sort through e-mails, faxes and phone conversations in search of certain keywords or other "flags." Other intelligence agencies apparently ask the NSA to flag specific words, phrases, organizations or people for surveillance purposes.

One report to the European Parliament charged that the United Kingdom used the Echelon project to spy on Amnesty International and the charity Christian Aid. (We should remember that George Orwell's novel *1984* depicted a totalitarian society in England, or "Oceana," not the Soviet Union.)

"Echelon can no longer be dismissed as an *X-Files* fantasy. The reports to the European Parliament make it quite clear that Echelon exists and that its operation raises profound civil liberties issues," said Barry Steinhardt, associate director of the ACLU.

So far, the NSA—aka "No Such Agency"—has refused to share with Congress the legal guidelines for the Echelon project, strangely citing "attorney-client privileges" for their silence. The U.S. House Government and Oversight Committee said it plans to hold hearings on Echelon. More important is the oversight of the mysterious and powerful NSA.

The 1948 U.K.-U.S.A. Agreement combined under a single umbrella group the SIGINT (signal intelligence) organizations of the United States, the U.K., Canada, Australia and New Zealand. The U.S. government under operation "Shamrock" began monitoring all international telegraph traffic during World War II, with no controls over what was inspected and what was not. During the Cold War, the Truman administration established the NSA to continue this function.

The NSA's birth at 12:01 a.m. on November 4, 1952, came without a public announcement. Born from a seven-page presidential memorandum signed by President Truman, the NSA is the largest, wealthiest, most powerful and least-known secret agency in our government. The agency's headquarters at Fort Meade, Maryland, is the second largest building in the U.S., eclipsed only by the Pentagon. In 1959, Congress passed a law forbidding the NSA to disclose any information about its activities, organization or names of employees. Ten years later, an investigative reporter estimated the NSA had 95,000 employees.

We do know in 1957 that the NSA initiated a five-year computer research program called Project Lightning. Out of this research came the Cray supercomputer. By 1977, reports surfaced that the NSA had the world's biggest collection of computers. The agency's in-house secret classification system goes one step higher than "top secret," with a classification titled "handle via comint channels only."

In 1967, David Kahn, a *Newsday* reporter and amateur code-breaker, wrote the book *The Code-breakers* that included a chapter on the NSA. This got Kahn's name placed on the NSA's notorious "watch list," enabling the agency to sweep all of Kahn's electronic communications. In his 1977 book, *Clearing the Air*, Daniel Schorr called the NSA "one of the deepest secrets" of our government. In 1982, James Bamford published a ground-breaking expose titled *The Puzzle Palace: A Report on America's Most Secret Agency.*

Reportedly, any journalist who dared write about the agency ended up on the watch list. To keep track of this small fraternity of investigators, NSA's in-house secret police agency M5 set up a special file called "Nonaffiliates of NSA Who Publish Writings Concerning the Agency," according to Bamford.

Bamford and other investigative reporters claim that the NSA began domestic espionage during the civil rights movement, which carried over to Vietnam War protesters in the '60s and '70s. President Nixon signed an addendum to the NSA's secret charter that sanctioned this previously unauthorized domestic surveillance, but President Jimmy Carter made a heroic attempt to restrict NSA activities.

The last Congressional investigation of the NSA by the Senate Intelligence Committee in 1978 noted that "the NSA's potential to violate the privacy of American citizens is unmatched by any other intelligence agency." The Congressional inquiry led to the Foreign Intelligence Surveillance Act of 1978.

The microelectronic revolution that's brought us cell phones and the Internet requires renewed scrutiny of the NSA. As Gregory T. Nojeim, the ACLU's legislative counsel, complained, "It appears that the U.S. government is once again spying on American's private communication. Congress must determine if Echelon is as sweeping and intrusive as has been reported, and most importantly, it must ensure that Americans' conversations are not intercepted without a court order."

December 2, 1999

Operation Blowback

The CIA's famous word for unintended consequences—"blowback"—explains it all: bin Laden, Al-Qaeda, the Taliban.

It's a good thing Americans are notoriously ahistorical. Otherwise they might remember how the U.S. installed Pakistani military dictator General Zia ul-Haq in 1977. They might also remember President Jimmy Carter's National Security Advisor, Zbigniew Brzezinski—wearing a bizarre turban that looked like it was borrowed from an Indian Sikh rather than an Afghan warrior—standing on the border of the Soviet Union and shouting to the Mujaheddin to "wage a jihad!" against the Communists. In the summer of 1979, Brzezinski advised Carter to sign a secret directive to support the fledgling Mujaheddin movement. That was six months before Soviet tanks rolled into Kabul.

In a series of articles and books, Brzezinski, a former Columbia University professor, analyzed how the multi-ethnic Soviet Union could be destroyed through inflaming the religious passions of 50 million to 60 million Central Asian Muslims. The Mujaheddin took the message to heart. They're now waging a jihad against us.

Soon after the anti-Soviet jihad began, Dan Rather, in more authentic headgear, broadcast live alongside what he called "Afghan freedom fighters...who were engaged in a deeply patriotic fight to the death for home and hearth."

Rather made heroes of Afghan opium runners like Yunas Khalis, who fought to control Afghanistan's poppy fields more than he fought the Soviets. Seven heroin labs near Khalis' headquarters in Ribat helped fund the jihad. U.S. taxpayers kicked in too, through the construction of an irrigation system in the Helmand Valley, where 60 percent of Afghanistan's opium grows.

The Reagan-Bush administration enthusiastically joined the jihad against the Soviets. The concomitant drugs and arms bazaar flourished in the northwest Pakistan town of Darra with America's loyal allies, the Pakistani Inter-Service Intelligence, regulating both the opium and arms trades to the Mujaheddin.

The U.S. government pressured China, Egypt and Saudi Arabia to support the covert operation. Egyptian President Anwar Sadat remarked shortly before his assassination by the Mujaheddin network that "The U.S. contacted me, they told me, 'Please open your stores for us so that we can give the Afghans the arms they need to fight.'" Sadat was the first famous casualty of the blowback.

The Saudi royal family, despite pressure, declined direct participation. Instead they sent Osama bin Laden—the son of one of Saudi Arabia's wealthiest citizens—to Afghanistan. Government records indicate the CIA's covert action in creating the Mujaheddin and bin Laden's terrorist apparatus cost $3.2 billion, the most expensive covert operation in the CIA's history.

So lucrative was the opium and drug business in the Golden Crescent—where Afghanistan, Pakistan and Iran meet—the off-shore accounts in Pakistan's largest bank, Habib, overflowed. The Bank of Credit and Commerce International (BCCI), founded by Agha Hasan Abedi, pitched in to help with the money laundering and became notorious as the most corrupt bank in world history. BCCI now stands for the Bank of Crooks and Criminals International, after going belly-up in 1991 with a reported $20 billion missing.

Well there's bound to be some wealth generated when, according to DEA documents, 40 heroin syndicates were operating in Pakistan in the mid-1980s through an estimated 200 heroin manufacturing facilities.

In May 1984, Vice President George Bush traveled to Pakistan to confer with our dictator, General Zia. Bush the Elder, the former CIA director, handed the drug problem over to the CIA, despite its notorious history of involvement with cocaine traffickers in Central America and heroin trafficking in Central Asia. Bush granted the CIA primary responsibility for controlling drug informants and other "assets" in the Golden Crescent.

By 1989, the Soviets were in full retreat from Afghanistan while bin Laden and his Mujaheddin and Taliban allies were firmly in control of heroin traffic in Central Asia. Bin Laden's biographer, Yossef Bodansky, said Osama envisioned BCCI as a "world bank for fundamentalists" before its collapse.

In 1992, the U.S. Senate's Foreign Relations Committee issued a massive report on the BCCI scandal. If you want to understand where bin Laden's money came from—though the media originally reported he inherited $300 million from his father, they've now correctly adjusted that to $20 million—you need to know of BCCI's role in the world of guns and drugs. You might want to start with Section 13 of the Senate report, titled "BCCI, the CIA and Foreign Intelligence."

Caught up in the scandal were Jimmy Carter's ethically challenged former Director of the Office of Management and Budget, Bert Lance, former Secretary of Defense Clark Clifford and other infamous individuals. The Senate's BCCI report recommended further investigation was needed into "international criminal financier Mark Rich." Remember Rich—the guy pardoned by Bill Clinton? The report states, "Rich's commodities firms were used by BCCI in connection with BCCI's involve[ment] in U.S. guaranteed programs through the Department of Agriculture."

Cincinnati's Charles Keating was included in two of the Senate committee's 20 recommendations for further investigation. The report noted, "The financial dealings of BCCI directors with Charles Keating and several Keating affiliates and front-companies, including the possibility that BCCI-related entities may have laundered funds for Keating to move them outside the United States."

BCCI funds also allegedly financed the controversial WTI incinerator in East Liverpool, Ohio, with the Swiss firm Von Roll. Four of Von Roll's top officials were convicted for selling material for the Iraqi "Supergun." Government documents also link WTI to Mafia families in the U.S. and the incinerator was involved in a political money-laundering scandal connected to Ohio Governor George Voinovich's administration.

The *Times of London* reported shortly after the September 11 attacks that Deloitte and Touche, the accounting firm, was being dragged into the hunt for Osama bin Laden's terror network. The *Times* reported that BCCI was used to launder terrorist money and as the chief depository for CIA covert funds paid to bin Laden during the Afghan war with the Soviets.

The *St. Louis Post-Dispatch* also noted, "Before it [BCCI] was shut down in 1991, it was used to fund the Mujaheddin, then fighting the Soviet-supported government of Afghanistan. The money came from U.S. and Saudi intelligence."

It's blowback time indeed.

November 1, 2001

OSU vs. Osama bin Laden

Prior to the campus unrest in the late '60s and early '70s, colleges were comfy spots to spy on people, conduct mind-control experiments and plot coups in the Third World. Midwest football coaches like OSU's fabled Woody Hayes could teach military science and encourage their "best boys" to join elite units like the Navy SEALS or work for the CIA.

All that was shattered when radical campus activists stormed administration buildings and looked through universities' top-secret files. It turns out Ohio State University was one of a dozen or so campuses that took part in the MK-Ultra mind-control experiments in the early to mid '60s through the university's psychology department.

Once the jig was up, social scientists began to refuse contracts for research that could lead to covert operations against Third World countries and their citizens; CIA spooks slunk off to research institutes and hid their connections to universities; and the House Un-American Activities Committee was disbanded and most of the Red Squads that spied on dissidents were renamed, downsized or destroyed.

But in the aftermath of September 11, the "war on terrorism" will be the excuse to settle an old score between the liberal campuses and military-industrial complex aficionados.

In April 2002, OSU announced that it's forming a "new

multi-disciplinary research program designed to assist federal and state officials in better understanding the causes of international terrorism and finding appropriate solutions."

The man in command is retired Air Force Major General Todd I. Stewart. He comes to Ohio State straight from Wright-Patterson Air Force Base near Dayton. You know, the place where they paid white airmen to breed prior to World War II in the nation's only acknowledged eugenics test; where Project Paperclip warmly welcomed Nazi scientists; a base shrouded in secrecy and rumors of strange high-tech military programs.

The OSU press release acknowledged, "The new program also represents a collaboration with the Battelle Memorial Institute." Great, the Dr. Strangelove Institute reunited on campus with the Wright-Pat guys. Perhaps they can reminisce about old Nazi scientists or Soviet defectors who were lab buddies in creating weapons of mass destruction and genetically altered silica-impregnated anthrax strains.

According to the OSU press release, "Stewart said his role initially will be to facilitate the process of identifying research efforts within the university that could influence national and international security and connect them with outside development entities such as Battelle."

Since Stewart's Program for International and Homeland Security is dedicated to understanding "the source of terrorism and solutions," perhaps it could start by studying the history of Battelle and Wright-Pat. Here's my suggestion for a model curriculum: Chemical and Biological Warfare 101; a seminar on How to Redirect the U.S. Nuclear Arsenal to Punish Rogue Nations; a lab on Hands-on Mind Control Techniques; and extra credit for taking some LSD.

The program could also publish its own newspaper to practice mass propaganda techniques. Come to think of it, somebody's got to do surveillance on all the faculty e-mails as part of the newly passed U.S. Patriot Act. Who better than the major general and his fatherland security students?

Unfortunately, I think Stewart's too much of a traditionalist to offer such a cutting-edge and honest curriculum. Stewart is a member of the Christian Embassy, a nondenominational ministry established in 1975 that focuses on bringing the word of Jesus to government officials. He led prayers for the group shortly after September 11. Stewart also presided over a half-time military ceremony that included two Air Force flyovers where 150 young people were sworn into the Air Force. Ah, bringing back the '50s.

Not to be outdone, Kent State University Professor Mitch Fadem pre-empted OSU's announcement by telling the *Akron Beacon Journal* that he's working "to attract $1 million in federal funding" to pursue his dream of spraying people with an anthrax vaccine.

The *Beacon Journal* conceded that Fadem's idea "sounds like the stuff of a Tom Clancy novel," but "the 50-year-old toxicologist envisions tests with a military transport airplane flying over a remote area of southern Canada and spraying a chemical compound on simulated anthrax."

Fadem stressed that he's already worked with the Air Force Reserve's 910th Airlift Wing at the Youngstown Air Reserve Station. The 910th is the U.S. military's only solely dedicated aerial spraying unit. Fadem, a captain in the reserve, hopes to use the "big tanks and nozzles attached to the C-130s to decontaminate an area exposed to chemical or biological agents," according to the *Beacon Journal*.

The *Beacon Journal* quotes Fadem as saying: "I've been telling people for a long time [bioterrorism] is going to happen here. The climate was right. I knew how open the United

States was and how easy it would be to get the materials."

Fadem has already conducted spraying tests in his labs "to determine the concentration that would kill the anthrax spores without harming people or damaging buildings." Two other Kent State professors are competing with Fadem by concentrating on killing anthrax via irradiation.

Fadem and his colleagues, like Stewart, are interested in the $2.8 billion earmarked for counter-terrorism research in the federal government's next budget. Well, at least a conservative president is finally funding higher education. This April 15, you might as well write your tax payment check directly to "Tom Ridge, Director of Homeland Security."

April 11, 2002

Blindfolded Intelligence

So U.S. leaders have finally decided to ask the obvious questions about the September 11 terrorist attacks. Since those events represent the most catastrophic intelligence failure in our nation's history, and since such incompetence invites charges of conspiracy or complicity by some, a thorough Congressional investigation is essential.

Let's go over the key facts one more time: Various other countries—including Israel, Russia, Germany and Egypt—warned the U.S. of an impending terrorist attack in the months prior to September 11. While lacking specific details, these warnings focused on the hijacking of commercial aircraft by terrorists.

For example, the German Intelligence Service told U.S. and Israeli intelligence agencies in June 2001 that terrorists were "planning to hijack commercial aircraft to use as weapons to attack important symbols of American and Israeli culture," according to the *Frankfurter Allgemeine Zeitung* newspaper. Moreover, the *Zeitung* reported that the U.S. knew of this information through its top-secret Echelon system of 120 satellites that monitors virtually all electronic data transmissions worldwide.

According to MSNBC and Russian news reports, Russian intelligence notified the CIA during the summer of 2001 that 25 terrorist pilots had been specifically training for suicide missions. In August, Russian President Vladimir Putin claims he warned the U.S. government "in the strongest possible terms" of impending attacks against government buildings and airports.

Despite disingenuous denials by the Bush administration, U.S. intelligence agencies and the military have been well aware of the possibility that planes could be used to bomb buildings. In 1993, the Defense Department's Office of Special Operations and Low-Intensity Conflict issued a report about just such a scenario.

That same year, renown futurist Marvin J. Cetron told military officials and terrorist experts at a Langley Air Force Base conference, "Coming down the Potomac, you could make a left turn at the Washington Monument and take out the White House, or you could take a right turn and take out the Pentagon." The next year, Cetron wrote, "Targets such as the World Trade Center not only provide the requisite casualties, but, because of their symbolic nature, provide more bang for the buck. In order to maximize their odds for success, terrorist groups will likely consider mounting multiple simultaneous operations."

Or if the terrorists couldn't go to Cetron's military briefing or read his article, they could simply buy American videogames and learn how to fly commercial jetliners into skyscrapers. The U.S. media is currently awash with talk of FBI agent Kenneth Williams' July 2001 memo warning that bin Laden's followers might be training in American flight schools and the CIA's 1999 analysis that bin Laden loyalists might crash a plane into the Pentagon or the White House.

Fueling the debate are a couple of curious written works published in the mid-'90s: former National Security Advisor Zbiginew Brzezinski's *The Grand Chessboard* and the U.S. Air Force's methodological chapter on "Alternative Futures" assessment. Both essentially outline how a terrorist attack on the U.S. could be a catalyst to rally the American people to achieve U.S. military world dominance. The Air Force called its scenario "Gulliver's Travails."

Thus, some are wondering how perhaps the most technologically advanced nation in the world—with the National Security Agency's Echelon, the FBI's Carnivore and Magic Lantern electronic eavesdropping systems and technology like Tempest that reportedly can detect a computer monitor display from over a block away—could have been so incompetent.

Former German Minister of Technology Andreas von Buelow raised a series of provocative questions in a January 2002 *Tagesspiegel* newspaper interview. Von Buelow places the September 11 events within the context of 26 U.S. intelligence services with a budget of $30 billion, and we can add to that another $13 billion or so in counter-terrorism money. As von Buelow sees it, "With the help of the horrifying attacks, the Western mass democracies were subjected to brainwashing. The enemy image of anti-Communism doesn't work anymore; it is to be replaced by people of Islamic belief."

Von Buelow points to Brzezinski and Samuel Huntington, the author of *The Clash of Cultures*, as advocates of those wishing to create an "enemy image." He calls Brzezinski a "mad dog" who believes it's the "exclusive right of the U.S. to seize all the raw materials of the world, especially oil and gas."

Brzezinski's book *The Grand Chessboard* articulates the need for the U.S. to take control of Central Asian oil in the former Soviet republics. In von Buelow's assessment, "The CIA, in the state interest of the U.S., does not have to abide by any law in interventions abroad, is not bound by international law."

"For 60 decisive minutes, the military and intelligence agencies let the fighter planes stay on the ground; 48 hours later, however, the FBI presented a list of suicide attackers," von Buelow continued. "Within 10 days, it emerged that seven of them were still alive… they made payments with credit cards with their own names; they reported to their flight instructors with their own names. They left behind rented cars with flight manuals in Arabic for jumbo jets. They took with them, on their suicide trip, wills and farewell letters, which fall into the hands of the FBI, because they were stored in the wrong place and wrongly addressed. Clues were left behind like in a child's game."

His advice to the American people: "Search for the truth!"

May 23, 2002

Anthrax Ground Zero

In the aftermath of the terrorist attacks on the World Trade Center and Pentagon, and a report that one of the terrorists trained on a crop-dusting plane, the media has increasingly turned its speculation of future horror to chemical and biological warfare.

A week after September 11, when the nation's nerves were still frayed, the *Cleveland Plain Dealer* rather alarmingly wrote: "With a dusting of anthrax spores from a helicopter or a mist of nerve gas in a subway ventilation system, terrorists could carry out a stealthy chemical or biological strike as lethal as the World Trade Center suicide mission."

Fortunately, here in central Ohio, we have the Battelle Memorial Institute to protect us.

Since 1979, the number of Battelle employees involved in chemical and biological warfare research at its King Avenue and West Jefferson laboratories has grown from 500 to 800, according to the *New York Times*.

In order to keep us safe from "terrorist attacks," Battelle is involved in manufacturing a more deadly strain of anthrax, the *Times* reported. As Battelle explained to the *Columbus Dispatch*, you have to develop the more deadly lethal strain so that a vaccine can be found. It's termed "defensive" work.

The *Times* also reported that to keep us safe from terrorism, the Central Intelligence Agency once replicated a Soviet-era biological bomb to study how well it would disperse biological agents like anthrax under varying atmospheric conditions. The *Times* said two sets of tests were conducted at Battelle.

The United States is reported to have the largest inventory of biological and chemical agents in the world. All are officially for defensive purposes. Assisting Battelle in its "defensive" biological weapons program is Dr. Kenneth Alibek, described in a 1998 *Dispatch* article as a former "top official in a massive Soviet effort to develop biological weapons for possible use against American forces."

The *Dispatch* reported that "Alibek was first Deputy Director Biopreparat, the civilian arm of the Soviet biological-weapons program." He supervised 3,200 workers in over 40 facilities. Following World War II, various former Nazi scientists reportedly worked at Battelle as a byproduct of Operation Paper Clip, a Cold War operation to secure Hitler's best and brightest before the Soviets snatched them.

The Russian government has charged that Battelle's activity violates a 1972 global treaty banning secret research on biological weapons. The 1972 protocol specifically forbids nations from developing or acquiring weapons that spread disease, but allows work on vaccines and other "protective measures." Since the CIA bomb was built and tested for purely "defensive" measures, the military denies it's violating the treaty.

The Jefferson Township Fire Department has assured West Jefferson and central Ohio residents that everything is safe. Fire Lieutenant Timothy Stainer told the *Dayton Daily News*, "We have had training specific to anthrax." The training drills occur four times a year.

Battelle's website notes, "The United States Department of Defense openly acknowledges the capacity of both potential adversaries and terrorists to employ weapons of mass destruction, particularly chemical and biological (CB) weapons... Battelle's CB defense product line is organized to support these programs."

I haven't felt this reassured about my safety since Ronald Reagan named our nuclear missiles "Peacekeepers." If Americans can't tell the difference between freedom-loving defensive anthrax and evil terroristic bin Laden-type anthrax, then they ought to just get the hell out of central Ohio.

September 27, 2001

Anthrax Money Trail

The spooky Dr. Strangelove Institute headquartered in Columbus may be ground zero in the domestic anthrax scare. With five people dead and 18 ill from the letter-borne biological agent, Battelle's role in directing the U.S. Defense Department's "joint vaccine acquisition program" is now coming under heavy scrutiny.

Battelle, in partnership with BioPort of Lansing, Michigan, has a virtual monopoly on military anthrax vaccine production in the United States. BioPort is partly owned by a top-secret British bio-warfare consortium, Porton International. The *New York Times* reported in July 1998 that BioPort's owners included Admiral William Crowe Jr., a former chair of the U.S. Joint Chiefs of Staff and ambassador to Britain during the Clinton years. One of Crowe's partners is the mysterious Fuad El-Hibri, a German citizen of Lebanese descent and a reported business associate of the bin Laden family.

Laura Rozen pointed out in a Salon.com article that El-Hibri, BioPort's CEO, "made a fortune" working for "Porton International" during the Gulf War a decade ago. Porton had a virtual monopoly on the anthrax vaccine in Britain in partnership with Battelle. Porton International's for-profit arm, the Centre for Applied Microbiology and Research (CAMR), announced in March 2001 it was putting together a joint proposal with Battelle to supply the U.K. with an anthrax vaccine.

What's Porton International, you might ask? Well, they're the Battelle, so to speak, of the U.K. In the weeks immediately preceding the September 11 attacks, the consortium's laboratories located at Porton Down made national news in Britain when the BBC reported that Porton Down scientists had conducted biological and chemical experiments on "about 20,000 so-called human guinea pigs... between 1939 and the 1960s."

In August 2001, Britain's *Independent* newspaper reported that Porton's chemical and biological defense branch "tested LSD on soldiers to investigate its 'tactical battlefield usefulness'" in the '60s. The *Sunday Telegraph* reported that the experiments included dripping liquid sarin, the deadly nerve gas, onto a patch taped to a soldier's arm. The British police were investigating between 45 and 70 deaths linked to the experiments.

As I reported in *Columbus Alive* immediately after the anthrax scare began, Battelle is involved in developing a new and stronger strain of anthrax at its West Jefferson labs. Don't be deceived by the fake farmland facades of the West Jefferson complex: It's the center of an unclassified defense project going under the name "Project Jefferson," according to the *New York Times*.

The *Times* also confirmed that the CIA is involved with its own top-secret anthrax project, code-named "Clear Vision." The presence of the CIA and specter of "national security" is thwarting the current FBI investigation into the mailed anthrax, sources say.

More than any other organization, Battelle controlled access to the Ames strain of anthrax used in various secret projects—and the strain found in the deadly letters. The *Baltimore Sun* reported that the Ames strain was also being produced at the Dugway Proving Ground in Utah, but this is a red herring. Battelle's involved in that program as well.

A December 2001 Battelle press release reads: "Battelle is expanding… with the opening of a suite of offices in West Valley City, Utah. The office will house existing business operation from Battelle's Dugway, Hill Air Force Base, and Toole, Utah, locations." Battelle co-manages many labs and projects including the Oak Ridge National Laboratory, well known for its role in the nuclear weapons industry.

As I previously noted, the number-two man in the former Soviet biochemical warfare operation, Kanatjan Alibekov—now going by the alias Ken Alibek—is a classified consultant with both the CIA and Battelle. A 1998 *New Yorker* article pointed to work on the anthrax project Alibek conducted with William C. Patrick III. Patrick, now president of Biothreat Assessments, has 48 years of biological warfare experience with the U.S. military, including a stint as the chief of the Army's Product Development Division (which weaponizes biological agents).

The current FBI investigation has led toward the Patrick/Alibek/Battelle/CIA connection. But whether the feds have the will, or the authority, to investigate spook central in Columbus is another question. The *New York Times* reported that the FBI already made an error in the "anthrax probe" by allowing the "destruction of university" samples that "may have caused clues to be lost."

London's *Telegraph* reported, under the headline "CIA links Porton Down to anthrax attacks," that "Sources in the FBI said the CIA was under investigation because of the bureau's 'interest' in a contractor which used to work for the agency in its anthrax program." Sources at Battelle and in law enforcement say the contractor in question was Alibek.

Alibek, who arrived in the U.S. in 1992, needs to be looked at very closely; news reports suggest he had possible financial stakes in a biochemical scare. On October 29, the *Washington*

Post reported that Alibek "has hooked up with an Alexandria, Virginia, company, and, supported by federal grants, opened a laboratory of 35 people." The article notes the former Soviet bio-warfare scientist is "learning to be a capitalist."

"Hadron Advanced Biosystems Inc., Alibek's company, sports an unusual provenance for a biotechnical venture. No other company, doing any kind of work, can claim to be headed by a former number-two man in a vast program aimed at turning anthrax, plague, smallpox, tularemia and many other germs into weapons of war," noted the *Post*. "Alibek's venture is a subsidiary of Hadron Inc…. a publicly traded 37-year-old government contractor specializing in defense and espionage work."

The FBI's investigation initially focused on who stood to gain financially from the deadly anthrax letters (as in, who has a stake in increased sales of the anthrax vaccine, for instance). Sources close to the investigation say that El-Hibri's possible ties to the bin Laden family also caused the FBI some concern—not to mention his role as CEO of the only laboratory in the U.S. licensed to sell the anthrax vaccine. But the convergence of the Strangelovian Battelle with BioPort, the British Porton Down consortium and the role of prominent individuals like Alibek, Crowe and El-Hibri suggests that much of this is likely to be covered up.

Ironically, in the summer of 2001 George W. Bush renounced long-standing calls by the Russians for mutual inspections of biochemical weapons sites like Battelle. Bush claimed that mutual inspection of U.S. biochemical technology sites by foreign scientists could risk revealing commercial trade secrets—secrets that would be worth a fortune if a few people controlled the commercial rights to them.

January 10, 2002

Bug Hunt

Central Ohio residents may occupy Ground Zero in the United States' secret bio-chemical war experiments. The national and international press have documented the Battelle Memorial Institute's connection to anthrax experiments and the Ames strain of the bug linked to the deadly mailings. Wayne Madsen's article "Thinking the Unthinkable," published by Counterpunch.org, nicely summed up the government's foot dragging (or cover up) in the anthrax case. Not surprisingly, the article refers to Battelle, which Madsen calls "a favorite Pentagon and CIA contractor."

Last year, in their book *Germs, New York Times* writers Judith Miller, Stephen Engelberg and William Broad described the key role of Battelle in both the military's and the CIA's Ames-strain anthrax projects: "Battelle, a military contractor in Columbus, Ohio, with sophisticated laboratories, conducted at least two sets of tests on a model of the biobomblet that measured, among other things, its dissemination characteristics and how it would perform in different atmospheric conditions."

The CIA did not seek the White House's blessing for its anthrax "bomb" project, called "Clear Vision," the *Times* writers noted. The tests were completed in mid-2000.

Germs informs us that the Defense Intelligence Agency (DIA) was working on Project Jefferson to manufacture a war-grade super-strain of anthrax. "To make the genetically modified anthrax, the DIA turned to Battelle, its contractor in Columbus which had also worked on Clear Vision," according to the book.

Battelle reportedly conducted the CIA anthrax tests at West Jefferson and the DIA's tests at the Dugway Proving Grounds in Utah. A December 2001 Battelle news release issued from their Columbus headquarters refers to "Battelle's Dugway, Hill Air Force Base and Toole, Utah locations."

A BBC *News Night* investigation "raised the possibility that there was a secret CIA project to investigate methods of sending anthrax through the mail which went madly out of control."

"The shocking assertion is that a key member of the covert operation may have removed, refined and eventually posted weapons-grade anthrax which killed five people," according to the BBC.

While President Bush initially hinted that the anthrax unleashed in the U.S. was possibly linked to al Qaeda, Iraq or, more recently, Cuba, Barbara Rosenberg of the Federation of American Scientists claims that the FBI is dragging its feet in the investigation because an arrest would prove embarrassing to the U.S. government.

The FBI questioned both William Patrick III and Ken Alibek, who worked for Battelle and the CIA as either employees or consultants. The *New York Times* asserted that Patrick authored a secret paper on the implications of sending anthrax through the mail. Patrick denies this, but the BBC made a similar assertion and noted that Patrick "had been a suspect" in the mailed-anthrax deaths.

BBC Science Editor Susan Watts asked Patrick, "Did you perpetrate these attacks?"

Patrick responded, "My goodness. I did not... I did not... I'm an American patriot."

A September 7, 2001, Associated Press report noted a "new strain" of extremely lethal anthrax had been recently developed. The BBC and *New York Times* claimed that Patrick's report had the U.S. anthrax program achieving an unprecedented anthrax concentration of one trillion spores per gram, twice that of the Russian anthrax program, which Alibeck earlier headed.

The BBC also reported that Battelle, where Alibeck served as biological warfare program manager in 1998, conducted a secret biological warfare test involving genetically modified anthrax in early September 2001 in Nevada.

Meanwhile, you might have missed the significance of a small Associated Press article about the acquittal of Wouter Basson, aka "Dr. Death," but the British and South African media have reported in great detail on the biological and chemical warfare program of South Africa's former apartheid government. The program was code-named Project Coast; Dr. Death ran the biochemical program at the Roodeplat Research Laboratories, north of Pretoria. The usual details emerged: The racist government and its top-secret lab maintained ties to the U.S. biowarfare facility at Fort Detrick and the British company Porten Down, which is under investigation for allegedly murdering U.K. citizens in biochemical experiments.

Basson's prosecutors claimed that Dr. Death concocted drugs designed to kill only black people, developed techniques to contaminate envelope flaps with anthrax and worked on using ecstasy as a form of crowd control. Basson, of course, countered that he was fighting the spread of "communism and godlessness" in Africa, according to the London *Guardian*.

Basson professed, in his fight against the atheistic forces of Marxism and Leninism, that he worked with the CIA in a project called Operation Banana based in El Paso, Texas. Dr. Death claims that the CIA allowed him to transport cocaine from Peru through Texas to South Africa to develop a new drug that would incapacitate anti-apartheid activists.

And, by the way, he was charged with being involved in a project to send anthrax through the mail, working with a U.S. research institute. Wonder who that might be?

April 25 and May 30, 2002

Murky Network

The body of investigative reporter Joseph Casolaro was found in Martinsburg, West Virginia, with his wrists slashed on August 10, 1991. Near the body was a six-word suicide note: "I'm sorry, especially to my son," reported London's *Daily Telegraph*.

Why would a newspaper in England care about the tragic death of an obscure freelance reporter?

Casolaro had told his friends and family that he'd found a "network of murky individuals—he called it the octopus—linked with several covert operations and dubious organizations, including BCCI, which he suspected was used to funnel funds for arms sales to Iran," the *Telegraph* wrote.

There were mysterious circumstances surrounding Casolaro's death: He was meeting with an unnamed source in a hotel confirming links between U.S. officials, arms sales to Iran, and the Bank of Credit and Commerce International (BCCI); his body was hastily embalmed without the family's permission, which hampered a criminal investigation; and he had told his family that if he was killed in an accident, not to believe it.

Who is the Octopussy that might be lurking in the Ohio River Valley? Perhaps we should start by asking shy Arkansas billionaire Jackson T. Stephens. After all, Stephens introduced BCCI from Pakistan to the United States and brought the WTI waste incinerator to East Liverpool, Ohio. Stephens would be a good sketch artist because he's seen some monstrous scandals in his day. Stephens' family firm is the largest privately owned investment bank outside Wall Street. In September 1977, President Jimmy Carter's Budget Director Burt Lance was forced to resign amid allegations about his bank dealings with Stephens (Stephens and Carter were classmates at the Naval Academy). In 1978, Stephens, Lance and BCCI were charged with violating U.S. security laws. The charges were dropped after the defendants promised not to violate security laws in the future, even though they admitted no guilt.

The *New York Post* reported in February 1992 that it was Stephens who enabled BCCI to gain a foothold in the U.S. and helped the fraud-plagued bank secretly acquire U.S. banks. In Peter Truell and Larry Gurwin's book *False Profits*, perhaps the best account of the BCCI scandal, the authors outlined how opium revenue from Afghanistan's Mujahedin fighting the Soviets ended up in the accounts of BCCI, founded by Agha Hasan Abedi. The *Post* reported that Stephens allegedly introduced Abedi to Lance shortly after Lance resigned.

In 1991, Lance testified that he urged Abedi to acquire a Washington bank holding company, but he denied any knowledge of BCCI's subsequent secret ownership of First American Bankshares. The *Post* reported that Securities and Exchange Commission documents from 1977 substantiate that the idea originated with Stephens.

During Bill Clinton's 1992 presidential run, Stephens and his son Warren boasted of raising more than $100,000 for the campaign. The Stephens family also owned a 38 percent share in Worthen National Bank that extended a crucial $2 million line of credit to Clinton in January 1992.

But Stephens' Ohio roots go further back. Waste

Technologies Inc. (WTI) was a Stephens subsidiary chartered in Arkansas in 1975. In January 1980, a Stephens employee and former East Liverpool resident, Don Brown, informed local officials that Stephens wanted to build the WTI incinerator on land recently acquired by the newly formed Columbiana Port Authority. A press release issued in July 1981 identified four firms including WTI, a subsidiary of Stephens Inc. of Little Rock, and Von Roll of America Inc., an affiliate of the Swiss firm Von Roll Limited. Four Von Roll officials were convicted in Switzerland for attempting to illegally sell "supergun" parts to the Iraqi government during the Gulf War. It also owned New Jersey Steel, a company with reputed mob ties.

The combined presence in the Ohio Valley of Von Roll and Stephens, with his BCCI links, should raise eyebrows in law-enforcement circles—particularly in light of allegations of campaign money-laundering involving former Ohio Governor George Voinovich and his brother Paul and Von Roll lobbyist Tony Fabiano.

Richard Kerr, the deputy director of Central Intelligence, told Congress that BCCI "was involved in illegal activities such as money-laundering, narcotics and terrorism." The CIA director called BCCI "the Bank of Crooks and Criminals International," and admitted it paid its contractors from its accounts.

A sting by federal agents on a BCCI bank in Tampa, Florida, led to a 1991 Congressional investigation that uncovered more than 100 cases linking BCCI to drug-money laundering. Still, critics of the BCCI investigation charge that the Justice Department limited the scope to Tampa. If federal authorities were allowed to follow BCCI's tentacles into Arkansas or the Ohio River Valley, they surely would have intersected with the national security and intelligence apparatus of the U.S.

As investigative reporters Alexander Cockburn and Jeffrey St. Clair conclude in their essential book *Whiteout: The CIA, Drugs and the Press*, a great American tragedy occurred when the CIA and Bill Clinton were able to turn the allegations of Contra gun- and drug-running at the Mina Arkansas airbase into "the darkest backwater of right-wing conspiracy theories."

The Mina allegations included Stephens, BCCI, Miami's Southern Air Transport, and then-Governor Clinton connected to the octopussy. In Ohio, we have Stephens, BCCI, Von Roll, Columbus' Southern Air Transport and former Governor Voinovich. Perhaps for symmetry, we should simply dismiss the similarities between the Octopussies to that of the urbane, over-intellectual, left-wing paranoia.

Try to tell that to Casolaro, may he rest in peace.

April 15, 1999

The Octopussy's Tentacles

The Octopussy lurks in the murky, polluted waters of the Ohio River Valley. Scarier than the fabled Loch Ness Monster is the shadowy, mostly clandestine network involving organized crime, powerful politicians, mysterious Arkansas billionaire Jackson T. Stephens, the notorious and defunct Bank of Credit and Commerce International (BCCI) and the infamous Waste Technologies Inc. (WTI) waste incinerator in East Liverpool, Ohio.

While campaigning at Ohio State University in February 2000, Democratic presidential hopeful Al Gore encountered Citizen Action activists shouting "What about WTI?" and "Keep your promises!"

Gore's broken promise to halt the start-up of the WTI incinerator is as famous in environmental circles as President George Bush's "Read my lips, no new taxes" pledge in 1988.

Hell, I was duped by Gore's promise myself in 1992. That year, I'd served as Jerry Brown's Midwest coordinator at the Democratic Party convention. When Greg Haas, the Clinton-Gore campaign coordinator, asked me to sign a letter to former Brown delegates and environmentalists urging them to support the "Dubba Bubba" ticket, I did.

My support for Clinton and Gore stemmed primarily from

Gore's statements at a Weirton, West Virginia, campaign stop in July 1992. "The very idea of putting WTI in a flood plain, you know it's just unbelievable to me," he said. "We don't need these incinerators... I'll tell you this, a Clinton-Gore administration is going to give you an environmental presidency to deal with these problems. We'll be on your side for a change instead of the side of the garbage generators."

The letter I signed on behalf of the Clinton-Gore campaign touted the ticket's dedication to the environment. Unlike the numerous campaign pledges that Clinton dismissed as "pillow talk" between his first election and inauguration, Gore seemed sincere in his pledge to keep the WTI incinerator from firing up.

In December 1992, Gore issued a press release stating, "Serious questions concerning the safety of an East Liverpool, Ohio, hazardous waste incinerator must be answered before the plant may begin operation." Gore called for a "full investigation" by the U.S. General Accounting Office and pledged that the Clinton-Gore administration would not issue the plant a test burn permit until these questions were answered.

Within a few weeks, Clinton and Gore had reversed their opposition to the giant waste incinerator. Ohio Citizen Action recounts the history of WTI in its current newsletter: "According to unconfirmed reports from well-placed sources, Clinton's EPA administrator-designate, Carol Browner, called Valdus Adamkus, director of U.S. EPA's Great Lakes office. She asked Adamkus to approve WTI's initial 'test burn' before January 20 [1992], so the incoming Clinton administration would not have to take responsibility for the decision."

By early January 1992, WTI had the OK from Adamkus for a test burn, even though 400 children attended East Elementary School only 1,100 feet away from the incinerator's stack, spewing lead, mercury and dioxin into the valley's air, and houses were as close as 320 feet away.

Why did Clinton and Gore renege on their promise? Ask billionaire Stephens, if you can find him. Stephens was the single largest financial backer of the '92 Clinton-Gore campaign. He raised a reported $100,000 in contributions that year and is widely credited as having saved the Clinton campaign by extending a $3.5 million line of credit through his bank during the dark days of the Gennifer Flowers sex scandal.

Stephens is also the man responsible for introducing both the Pakistani bank BCCI to the United States and WTI to the Ohio River Valley.

Also involved with WTI is Von Roll of America Inc., an affiliate of the Swiss firm Von Roll Limited. Von Roll lobbyist Tony Fabiano was recently fined by the Ohio Elections Commission for money-laundering violations related to Governor George Voinovich's 1994 re-election campaign and also pleaded guilty to tax charges related to his role in securing environmental permits from the defunct North Ohio Valley Air Authority for WTI.

That WTI should play such a prominent role in both national Democratic and Ohio Republican scandals should come as no surprise. The *Wall Street Journal* reported in 1991 that Stephens arranged a bailout for a small Texas oil company on the verge of bankruptcy. One of the company's directors and stockholders is also running for president—George W. Bush.

Beware the murky waters of the Ohio River Valley, where the secrets of BCCI, WTI and other monsters dwell. Be afraid of the Octopussy, be very afraid.

February 10, 2000

Deals For Dubya

Trying to make sense of George W. Bush's days in the oil business and his bizarre Harken Energy stock transactions? Well, if you dig deep enough, you'll find a core group of people surrounding the notorious Bank of Credit and Commerce International (aka Bank of Crooks and Criminals International).

BCCI was, among other nefarious things, the bank of choice for al Qaeda, the CIA, Saddam Hussein and Manuel Noriega. This spooky collection of opium warlords, Arab sheiks, Pakistani financiers and organized crime bosses perpetrated perhaps the greatest banking fraud in world history. BCCI's global criminal conspiracy was aided by connections to Washington insiders like the Bush family, former secretary of defense and CIA co-founder Clark Clifford, Senator Orrin Hatch and President Jimmy Carter.

Award-winning journalists Peter Truell and Larry Gurwin document Dubya's ties to al Qaeda's favorite bank in their authoritative tome, *False Profits: The Inside Story of BCCI, the World's Most Corrupt Financial Empire.*

Truell, a *Wall Street Journal* reporter, and Gurwin, who broke the infamous Banco Ambrosiano scandal in the early 1980s, point out that both Bush political brothers Jeb and Dubya had close links to BCCI. Jeb socialized with Abdur Sakhia, BCCI's Miami branch manager and later the bank's top U.S. official.

Jeb's real estate company, Bush Klein Realty, managed the Grove Island complex of luxury condominiums where Sakhia lived. BCCI financed various real estate deals at the complex.

But, as Truell and Gurwin note, "George W. Bush had even closer ties to the BCCI network." In order to understand Bush's bogus Horatio Alger claims of being a struggling West Texas oilman who struck it rich and the later Harken stock shenanigans now in question, people need to look beneath the mythology and political spin.

As three-time Pulitzer Prize nominee Molly Ivins explains, "There's one thing to keep in mind as you read the many stories about George W. in the oil patch... He never found a revenue stream—unless you count investor's dollars flowing from New England to New York into the alkaline West Texas soil."

"The governor's oil-field career can be summed up in a single paragraph. George W. arrived in Midland in 1977, set up a shell company, lost a Congressional election in 1978, restarted building the company he'd put on hold, lost more than $2 million of other people's money, and left Midland with $840,000 in his pocket," Ivins offers in *Shrub: The Short But Happy Political Life of George W. Bush.*

Both Ivins and her co-writer Lou Dubose and the tandem of Truell and Gurwin concur that to assess Dubya's dubious business dealings, you've got to understand the role of rich and powerful family friends who were losing money in energy stock investments but speculating in Bush political futures.

When Dubya organized Arbusto Energy Inc. in the 1970s, James R. Bath, a well-known Texas businessman, provided some of the financing. During George Bush senior's tenure as CIA director, the agency allegedly used Bath, a business associate of the Saudi Khalid Bin Mahfouz—described by Truell and Gurwin as a "BCCI insider"—to buy CIA planes from Air America and other secretly held agency airlines.

Public records show that in 1976 the CIA sold several planes to Skyway, a firm managed by Bath. Bath denies it, but his former business partner Bill White has alleged the CIA's role in Skyway in lawsuits and also attested that Bin Mahfouz was an owner of Skyway.

Criminal and civil suits against BCCI established that Bath invested money on Bin Mahfouz's behalf and that he and Bin Mahfouz were part owners of Houston's Main Bank with Ghaith Pharaon, the son of a royal advisor to Saudi Arabia's King Faisal.

Dubya's undercapitalized and floundering Arbusto received badly needed cash from an old Princeton pal of Bush political advisor James Baker, Philip Uzielli, who paid $1 million for a 10 percent share in a company valued at $382,376. "Uzi," who made a fortune in Panama as the CEO of Executive Resources, claims he met Bush senior when he was CIA director.

In the mid 1980s, Arbusto hit hard times and merged with another desperate oil company to form Spectrum 7 Energy Corporation. Harken Energy Corporation, called by *Time* magazine "one of the most mysterious and eccentric outfits ever to drill for oil," rescued Dubya's failing enterprise in a stock swap with Spectrum 7 in 1986. Dubya received nearly $600,000 worth of Harken stock, joined its board of directors and became a $120,000-a-year "consultant" for Harken. The next year, Harken stayed afloat through debt restructuring and was in the same sad financial shape as the earlier Spectrum 7 and Arbusto.

But Harken dramatically reversed its ill fortune in January 1990. As Truell and Gurwin explain, "Harken Energy was awarded one of the most coveted oil deals in the world: a concession to drill for crude oil off the coast of Bahrain. The decision stunned many people in the industry. Harken was not only a small firm, it had never drilled outside the United States, nor had it drilled offshore. The only explanation that made sense to many oil executives, was that the Bahrain government wanted to do a favor for the family of President Bush."

Coincidentally, Bush the Elder enjoyed similar success in the early '60s when his small oil company, later listed in a public document as a CIA proprietary, received a lucrative contract to drill the first deep-water oil wells off the shores of Kuwait.

Harken's Bahrain deal sharply drove up the price of the company's stock. By June 1990, Dubya had bailed and sold two-thirds of his Harken shares—a transaction he improperly failed to disclose to the Securities and Exchange Commission for several months. Dubya made $318,430 in profit on the sale. In August, Iraq invaded Kuwait and Harken stock fell by 25 percent, from $4 to $3 a share.

Harken creditors were threatening to foreclose unless debt payments were made, according to *U.S. News and World Report.* "Substantial evidence [existed] to suggest that Bush knew Harken was in dire straits," the magazine reported. Under U.S. law, insiders like Dubya are required to publicly report when they liquidate large blocks of stock. Bush reported his Harken stock sale eight months after the federal deadline, according to the *Wall Street Journal.*

"A extraordinary number of people connected to Harken or the oil deal have ties to BCCI," Truell and Gurwin conclude. In *False Profits,* they document that Harken's investment banking firm Stephens Inc. was the same firm that helped BCCI's founder Agha Hasan Abedi secretly and illegally buy up stock in First American Bank. Bahrian's Prime Minister Sheikh Khalifa bin-Salman al-Khalifa was both a BCCI stockholder in

1990 and instrumental in awarding Harken Bahrain's offshore drilling contract.

Another of Harken's large shareholders was Sheikh Abdullah Taha Bakhsh, whose principal banker was BCCI's Bin Mahfouz. Also, Harken board member Talat Othman, Bakhsh's investment manager, visited the White House on three separate occasions to discuss Middle East policy with President Bush the Elder.

Senator John Kerry's BCCI investigatory committee established that BCCI was a conduit for opium money laundering from the Golden Crescent where Afghanistan, Iran and Pakistan come together. The Arab oil sheiks were fronts to create the illusion of "petro dollars" funding the bank. Dubya and Harken Energy's friends at BCCI were the core of a group of people—supported by the CIA, the Pakistani Inter-Service Intelligence agency and the Saudi royal family—secretly funding the al Qaeda terrorist network and Islamic fundamentalist groups in their successful campaign to destroy the Soviet Union.

August 29, 2002

Spook Air

Something's rotten at Rickenbacker Port Authority. Maybe it's just the stench of the bankrupt corpse of Southern Air Transport, or the moldering smell of the $3 million the state pumped into the notorious airline before it folded.

Ohio taxpayers are among the more than 800 creditors now lined up to file claims against "Spook Air." SAT filed for bankruptcy in Columbus on October 1, 1998, the same day the Central Intelligence Agency Inspector General issued a report linking the cargo hauler to allegations of drug-running in connection with U.S.-backed Contra rebels in Nicaragua in the 1980s.

Once lauded as a coup for central Ohio development, landing Southern Air Transport's business at Rickenbacker eventually turned into a nightmare, as the enterprise became mired in massive debt and was closed under a cloud of suspicion about its true activities. Just how and why one of the world's most notorious airlines ended up in Columbus in the mid-1990s is a story that hasn't been fully examined until now.

Through a Freedom of Information Act request, *Columbus Alive* obtained a massive number of documents from the Rickenbacker Port Authority and additional records from the Ohio Department of Development showing that the Franklin County Commissioners and the Voinovich administration

46

offered hard-to-refuse incentives to get SAT's business, despite the airline's shady history.

"We are proud of Rickenbacker's growth and believe the addition of Southern Air Transport would represent a significant step forward," Franklin County Commissioner Arlene Shoemaker wrote Southern Air President William G. Langton in January 1995. SAT officials pitched a proposal involving the construction of a 180,000-square-foot corporate headquarters and air-maintenance facility on leased land in the Rickenbacker Air Industrial Park. They projected the total cost of the project at more than $36 million, and predicted the creation of 300 new jobs within a three-year period.

"I will need and look forward to help from the State of Ohio, the Port Authority, Franklin County, the City of Columbus, the Chamber of Commerce and any other groups or individuals you would suggest, to help effectuate a seamless move to Columbus, Ohio, and the Rickenbacker International Airport," wrote Langton in a February 1995 letter to the port authority's Executive Director Bruce Miller. A "seamless move," in Langton's estimation, would cost $3 million.

The port authority and the Ohio Department of Development, under the aegis of Governor George Voinovich's then-Chief of Staff Paul Mifsud, developed an attractive incentive package for SAT. The state development department agreed to provide SAT with a low-interest $6 million loan. The department promised an additional half-million dollars from a Business Development Capital Account to defray the cost of "eligible equipment associated with the project."

The Ohio Department of Transportation agreed to enter into a lease to support $10.2 million in Certificates of Participation to enable Rickenbacker to make "necessary taxiway and parking improvements to allow SAT to locate in the park," according to an SAT document. Such airport improvements are usually funded by the Federal Aviation Administration.

The document goes on to spell out that "the Rickenbacker Port Authority has committed approximately $600,000 to fund other public infrastructure improvements associated with the project... In addition, the port authority has also agreed to make available to SAT up to $30 million in port authority revenue bonds for eligible project related costs."

The SAT document noted, "Franklin County has also committed to granting a 100-percent abatement for 15 years on real property improvements under Ohio's Community Reinvestment Area Law."

News accounts show that The Limited owner Leslie Wexner played a role in SAT's relocation to Rickenbacker. Two other key figures in the SAT story have Columbus connections: Alan D. Fiers Jr., a starting tackle on the 1961 Ohio State University football team and a Buckeye assistant coach in 1962, who later became the chief of the CIA Central American Task Force; and retired Air Force Major General Richard Secord, head of air logistics for the CIA-owned Air America's covert action in Laos between 1966 and 1968, and air logistics coordinator in the illegal Contra re-supply network for Oliver North in the '80s.

Both Fiers and Secord eventually were found guilty of charges in connection with the Iran-Contra affair. In July 1991, Fiers pleaded guilty to two misdemeanor charges involving illegally supplying weapons to the Contras. According to the recent CIA report on Southern Air Transport, Fiers informed U.S. Senate investigators that the CIA told the DEA early on about Contra leaders being involved in drug smuggling.

Secord, who is a 1954 graduate of Columbus' South High

School, pleaded guilty in 1989 to a felony charge in connection with the cover-up of the Iran-Contra affair.

While SAT was busy setting up offices in central Ohio, the CIA was linking the airline to illicit activities. The October 1998 CIA report on Southern Air Transport says that as early as January 1987, the customs office in New Orleans was investigating an allegation of drug trafficking by SAT crew members. The 1987 memorandum noted that the source of the allegation was a senior FDN (Contra) official, and indicated that the official was concerned that "scandal emanating from Southern Air Transport could rebound badly on FDN interest including humanitarian aid from the United States."

The memo continues, "A February 23, 1991, DEA [Drug Enforcement Agency] cable to CIA linked SAT to drug trafficking. The cable reported that SAT was 'of record' in DEA's database from January 1985-September 1990 for alleged involvement in cocaine trafficking. An August 1990 entry in DEA's database reportedly alleged that $2 million was delivered to the firm's business sites and several of the firm's pilots and executives were suspected of smuggling 'narcotics currency.'"

How did such a notorious company come to set up shop in central Ohio? Perhaps it was the efforts of Langton to keep the airline's history in intelligence operations at arm's length that assured Ohio officials of SAT's success. In March 1995, Langton told the *Columbus Dispatch* that his company was "no longer connected to the CIA."

It remains unclear exactly why Franklin County Commissioners were so willing to bring the scandal-ridden airline to central Ohio. Commissioner Dorothy Teater told *Columbus Alive* that she was not aware of Southern Air's ties to the CIA.

"If it's true, that's awful," she said, adding the push to land SAT in Ohio came from the state Department of Development. "We commissioners were an afterthought. They asked us at the last second to sit in the audience at the press conference."

When asked last week if she was aware of SAT's past CIA links or allegations of drug running, Commissioner Shoemaker answered, "Certainly not."

Documents obtained by *Columbus Alive* show that local officials did not balk at the notion of an enterprise at one time linked to drug smuggling and covert operations worldwide setting up shop here. They were apparently willing to overlook any danger signals in an effort to please local commercial enterprises that might benefit from SAT business. In 1996, SAT spokesperson David Sweet told *Columbus Alive* the airline moved to Ohio because "the deal [put together by the development department] was too good to turn down."

The Franklin County Commissioners created the Rickenbacker Port Authority in 1979 in order to utilize excess military land at Rickenbacker Air Force Base for industrial, distribution and air cargo purposes. In February 1992, the county commissioners created a Community Reinvestment Area for five years, making the Rickenbacker Port Authority a lucrative investment zone.

In a 1994 corporate report, which *Columbus Alive* retrieved from the Rickenbacker Port Authority's files, Langton downplayed the airline's controversial past and its crucial role in the Iran-Contra scandal, describing it as "an all-cargo airline operating schedule, charter and wetlease service for shippers, freight forwarders, the Department of Defense, relief organizations and individual customers around the world."

In April 1994, William B. Holley, executive vice president for economic development for the Columbus Chamber of

Commerce, wrote the Ohio Job Creation Tax Credit Authority under the Ohio Department of Development, urging that the airline receive tax credits for relocating from Miami, Florida, to Rickenbacker International Airport in Columbus.

Edmund James, president of James and Donohew Development Services, told the *Columbus Dispatch* that negotiations with Southern Air had begun "exactly one year ago today," speaking at the March 16, 1995, press conference announcing that SAT was locating to Columbus. He let it be known that "much of the Hong Kong-to-Rickenbacker cargo will be for The Limited." James said, "This is a big story for central Ohio. It's huge, actually."

The day following the press conference, Brian Clancy, a cargo analyst with MergeGloban Inc., was quoted in the *Journal of Commerce*: "Limited Inc., the nation's largest retailer, is based in Columbus, a fact that undoubtedly contributed in large part to Southern Air's decision."

That same day, the *Dispatch* noted a meeting between Langton, Governor Voinovich and "other officials yesterday to discuss the air cargo carrier's plans."

Governor Voinovich is quoted saying, "This will be a new window to the world for Ohio business... It will be a boon for exports." Within a week, SAT announced it would be flying twice-weekly freighters from Hong Kong to Columbus on behalf of The Limited.

In an article titled "Touchdown in Columbus," SAT's company newsletter featured an artist's rendering of the proposed state-of-the-art headquarters on its cover and lauded "the very pro-business attitude of the State of Ohio and City of Columbus."

That pro-business attitude is evident in a 1995 letter from SAT's Langton to the Rickenbacker Port Authority. Although in response to *Alive*'s records request, former Governor Voinovich's staffers claimed no records exist linking the governor or then-Chief of Staff Mifsud to the SAT deal, a February 22, 1995, letter from SAT chief Langton to Miller of the port authority stated: "I was very pleased with my visit with Mr. Paul Mifsud and Governor Voinovich, and after meeting with the State of Ohio it is my understanding that they will make the appropriate changes in funding amounts that we require in our Response to Proposal... I would expect to have a decision on the matter on or before March 10, 1995." Numerous other SAT correspondence were carbon-copied to Mifsud at the governor's office.

Repeated calls and a fax sent to Senator Voinovich's office seeking comment were not answered.

The next day, a letter from Ohio Department of Development Director Donald Jakeway to Langton begins, "Pursuant to your recent meeting with this department and Paul Mifsud, we are responding with this revised commitment letter..." Jakeway outlined a "revised preliminary commitment" worth an estimated $7.2 million in services, benefits, tax credits and low-interest infrastructure loans.

Jakeway is no longer with the Department of Development and was out of the country this week and could not be reached for comment. Calls to the Department of Development for comment were not returned.

In March 1995, Langton joined then-Governor Voinovich and officials from the Rickenbacker Port Authority to announce officially the relocation of SAT from Miami to Columbus. In the *Columbus Dispatch*'s coverage of the announcement, an exuberant Voinovich gushed, "I am extremely pleased to welcome Southern Air Transport to Ohio, as it will be the first airline to have its world headquarters located at

Rickenbacker Airport. This will help Columbus tremendously in becoming a world-class inland port."

Shoemaker, representing the Franklin County Commissioners, said, "We're deeply grateful to the governor and all those who helped make it possible to welcome Southern Air to Franklin County."

Langton called Rickenbacker "an opportunity waiting to happen."

By the end of the year, Langton was not sounding quite so positive. In the SAT newsletter, he stated: "As we close out 1995, I am sorry to report that we have the first loss year in recent history for Southern Air Transport."

Apparently, the airline was in better shape financially when it was engaged in covert and possibly illegal activities. Officials of SAT, which was founded in 1947, acknowledge that their airline was owned by the CIA from 1960 to 1973. In 1960, the CIA purchased SAT for $300,000 and rapidly expanded the airline's business into the Far East and Latin America. At one point, SAT was the CIA's largest "proprietary"—a private business owned by the CIA—with estimated assets of more than $50 million and more than 8,000 employees worldwide.

In 1973, the CIA sold SAT to "the official who had run it on behalf of the CIA, with a $5.1 million loan from First National Bank of Chicago, known to be a CIA-used bank," according to the *National Journal*.

The airline retained informal ties with both the CIA and the National Security Council. The current principal owner is Miami attorney James Bastian, former CIA lawyer, who chaired the investment partnership of the management group that acquired SAT from the CIA. In 1979, Bastian acquired the company's outstanding stock.

The airline's activities after that suggest that it was still heavily tied to the U.S. national security apparatus. During the 1980s, Southern Air Transport carried a variety of military supplies, arms and equipment to the Contras. Southern Air President Langton admitted in an affidavit in the civil trial of SAT employee Eugene Hasenfus that SAT flew TOW anti-tank missiles from Kelly Air Force Base in San Antonio, Texas, to Israel. Southern Air crews then loaded the missiles onto Israeli-owned planes that flew them into Iran.

At the time, President Ronald Reagan was officially urging the world to embargo Iran, a country he called "Murder, Inc." In 1986, SAT secretly shipped 90 tons of TOW missiles to Iran as part of the Reagan administration's secret arms-for-hostages exchange. Proceeds from the sale of the missiles—some $16 million—were diverted to the Contra re-supply effort in Central America. The scandal broke when on October 5, 1986, a Southern Air Transport C-123 cargo plane carrying 10,000 pounds of arms was shot down over Nicaragua.

The flight logs of the downed Southern Air Transport C-123 linked it to a history of involvement with the CIA, cocaine and the Medellin drug cartel in Colombia. The logs documented several Southern Air Transport flights to Barranquilla, Colombia, during October 1985, the same time Wanda Palacios, a Miami FBI informant, told the FBI that the airline was running drugs.

(It was also the same airplane that Louisiana drug dealer Barry Seal used in a joint CIA-DEA sting operation in 1984 against the Sandinistas. Seal acquired the plane through a complicated airline swap with the Medellin cartel, according to declassified government documents, and the plane was fitted with hidden cameras by the CIA at Rickenbacker Air Force

Base. Seal reportedly flew weapons for the Contras and returned to the United States with cocaine. He was murdered in New Orleans in 1986 by Colombian hitmen.)

Reports of SAT involvement with drug runners surfaced early on in the Congressional Iran-Contra inquiry. In August 1987, the *New York Times* reported Palacios informed Congressional investigators that "she witnessed drugs being exchanged for guns intended for the Contras." Palacios identified Southern Air Transport planes involved in the gun and drug running in two separate incidents in 1983 and 1985. Initially SAT denied any connection to the CIA and dismissed accusations of drug running as absurd.

Although SAT issued an internal memo denying any post-Iran-Contra connections to the CIA, during the Gulf War in 1990-91 Southern Air Transport played a key role in logistic support for the U.S. military. And in September 1990, the Air Force awarded SAT a $54 million contract for "air transport services."

Early 1996 opened for SAT with the same story when it garnered a 90-day contract to transport construction supplies, equipment and civilian personnel from Zagreb, Croatia, to Tuzla, Bosnia, one of the world's military hot spots.

By the end of January 1996, company officials assured the *Dispatch* that SAT "isn't backing away from the central Ohio hub," but SAT officials were dragging their feet on plans to begin construction on a hangar at Rickenbacker.

SAT's lack of action did not stop the state's Controlling Board from approving, in May 1996, a half-million-dollar grant "related to the overall project of constructing a 180,000-square-foot facility." Documents show that Doug Talbott of the Ohio Department of Development hand-carried a $500,000 check to an SAT official on August 5, 1996.

In December 1996, the *Dispatch* reported that SAT was "delinquent in paying a $277,000 personal property tax bill." SAT spokesperson David Sweet insisted that "the company is financially sound and intends to proceed with its Rickenbacker plans. 'It's not that we don't have the money to pay the tax; we just dispute the amount,'" according to the *Dispatch*.

Langton, SAT's president of 15 years, left abruptly in March 1997, handing the reins back to the airline's owner James Bastian. Eight months later, SAT issued layoff notices to 100 of its 750 employees. Two months after that, Southern Air Transport publicly announced it would lay off 54 of the 65 maintenance workers at Rickenbacker and 43 of the 175 employees at the company's temporary headquarters on Kimberly Parkway. Rickenbacker Port Authority now lacked any airport maintenance facility.

SAT, which had promised 300 new jobs within three years—and had already taken at least $3.5 million in state money—admitted that it hadn't begun work on the maintenance facility project it had promised.

Marlo B. Tannous, deputy chief legal counsel for the Department of Development, issued a memo trying to figure out what "the exact job numbers" were submitted by SAT to the state. In June 1998, SAT announced it planned "to park and sell off most of its fleet of Lockheed Hercules L-100" planes.

That same month, Joseph C. Robertson, director of the state Department of Development, wrote J. Robert Peart, the executive vice president and CEO of SAT, inquiring about the $500,000 grant and an earlier $200,000 grant for new employee training. "It is critical that DOD receive an accurate assessment of your company's situation related to these agreements," Robertson wrote.

On July 30, 1998, Daniel F. Dooley, the chief financial officer of SAT, informed Lewie A. Main of the Department of Development that "Southern Air's project will not proceed as planned at Rickenbacker due to severe financial difficulty."

Fine Air Services of Miami announced a plan to purchase the financially troubled SAT on July 23, 1998. Robert Dahl, a consultant with Air Cargo Management Group, summed up SAT's financial woes by pointing out "there are fewer belligerent circumstances in the world today than there were during the Cold War." Apparently Spook Air needed the Soviets and the Red Menace to survive. Fine Air backed out of the agreement to purchase SAT "after getting a closer look at its books," according to the *Journal of Commerce*.

Kitty Hawk Inc., the world's largest operator of air cargo planes, signed a letter of intent shortly thereafter to buy SAT. Three weeks later, Kitty Hawk terminated the agreement. Neither Fine Air or Kitty Hawk gave reasons for their decisions not to purchase Southern Air.

Blanca Hernandez, a Southern Air spokesperson, denied rumors that the company was going to seek bankruptcy protection after the Kitty Hawk deal fell through. Three days later, Southern Air Transport grounded all its flights and fired 450 employees. Hernandez admitted that the company was "considering ways to liquidate assets." The *Dispatch* reported that the Ohio Department of Transportation would not try to "recoup" $3 million it had loaned SAT.

Telephone calls to Southern Air Transport seeking comment for this story were referred to Columbus attorney Randy Latour. Citing pending litigation, Latour declined to comment.

The *Dispatch* managed to put a positive spin on the death of Spook Air: "But there were plenty of good times for Southern Air. Its Hercules fleet became the pack mules of the skies, transporting odd-size cargo, including Keiko, the whale, and taking part in humanitarian airlifts to Bosnia and Somalia." Like local officials, the *Dispatch* ignored the mounting evidence of SAT's ties to cocaine smuggling.

More recently, the *Dispatch* reported that the airline's already messy bankruptcy may be further complicated by allegations that $32 million in the private account of SAT owner Bastian's wife Mary Bastian are company funds.

On October 1, 1998, the CIA Inspector General issued his report outlining allegations of Southern Air Transport's involvement in drug-running. That same day, Spook Air filed for bankruptcy in Columbus.

April 22, 1999

SAT Flies Again

"Former" CIA airline and bankrupt cargo carrier Southern Air Transport (SAT) has risen zombie-like from its grave to again stalk the Earth. According to a May 1999 story in the trade publication *Aviation Daily*, the newly created Southern Air Inc. has acquired "SAT's route authority and some of its assets."

The original SAT went bankrupt in October 1998 amidst allegations of cocaine and gun running. The new company—that's Southern Air Inc., not Southern Air Transport—is referred to as "the Columbus, Ohio-based company, formed May 10."

Alas, finally something to make us a world-class city. I hear these guys got connections, and I do mean *big* connections, all over the globe. The brand-spankin'-new Southern Air Inc. wants the U.S. Department of Transportation "to transfer SAT's certificates and exemptions to Southern so Southern can begin all-cargo service about September 1," *Aviation Daily* says.

This is curious. Court papers claim that SAT's Air Cargo Division lost more than $39 million in 1997, the year before it filed bankruptcy. Now who the hell would invest in a company that bleeds that kind of red ink?

We'll never know, if Southern Air Inc. has its way. They've asked the transportation department "for confidential treatment of investors."

Of course, the cargo carrier has a long history of providing confidentiality to investors and clients. Like the CIA, which owned SAT from 1960 to 1973. Or Ollie North and Richard Secord's Enterprise, which reportedly used the airline to arm both the Ayatollah Khomeni and resupply the Contras in Nicaragua. Or the alleged crack dealers who used the airline, according to the Drug Enforcement Agency, U.S. Customs and the CIA Inspector General.

If the old clients are worried about new practices getting the way, rest assured that "Southern plans to provide its own flight crew training." Southern Air has always focused on providing planes, crews, maintenance and insurance under long-term contracts to airlines and cargo companies in need of its specialized expertise. This practice is known in the industry as "wet leasing."

With the proper lubrication provided from secret investors, Southern Air Inc. is once again positioned to take over SAT's route, come rain or sleet or snow, or more snow.

June 3, 1999

SAT's Covert Cousin

Here's good news for Franklin County's Rickenbacker Port Authority: As of the spring of 1999, McMinnville, Oregon-based Evergreen International Airlines is increasing its scheduled cargo flights into the county's Rickenbacker International Airport.

You recall that the notorious Southern Air Transport went belly up in October 1998. The CIA-connected SAT was lured to Rickenbacker by the county and state at great expense to taxpayers—some $6 million in low-interest state loans, a 100-percent county tax abatement, and other incentives. The same day SAT filed for bankruptcy, a CIA Inspector General's report was released linking SAT to drug trafficking.

Evergreen, on the other hand, has had "two regularly scheduled flights from Hong Kong to Rickenbacker" since 1989, according to the *Columbus Dispatch*. Heck, why don't we just starts passing out taxpayer money right now to Evergreen? You know, grants, tax abatements, tax-increment financing, Enterprise Zone dollars, training money, low-interest loans—the works.

I just thank God we live in a city that is worthy of the almighty, faithful Evergreen Airlines. Let me repeat: Evergreen is nothing, and I mean *nothing*, like Southern Air Transport.

Well, except perhaps for the minor matter of connections to the Central Intelligence Agency.

Now, we shouldn't be concerned just because the Associated Press reported in 1980 that Evergreen Airlines was created when "Evergreen Helicopters of McMinnville bought Intermountain Aviation of Marana, Arizona, from the CIA in 1975 and used its assets to form Evergreen Airlines."

Nor should we worry about a little thing like Evergreen being created from a former CIA-owned company—a "proprietary"—as SAT was. Evergreen assured the public in 1980, right after the airline flew the deposed Shah of Iran—installed by the CIA in 1953—from Panama to Egypt, that "there is no current link between...[the] company and the CIA."

I know what you cynics, agitators and conspiracy theorists are thinking: Isn't that the same thing SAT told us before swiping millions from the Ohio state and Franklin County treasuries?

Jim Bastian, who owns SAT, had been identified in news reports as a CIA operative, while a 1980 AP report only referred to "George A. Doole, who has been identified as a prime figure in the CIA's aviation operations in the early '70s, has served as a consultant to Evergreen Helicopters."

We're lucky to have such a company in Columbus. Evergreen Helicopters is a legendary company, growing from one helicopter in 1969 to a $100 million worldwide operation with a thousand employees in a decade.

Pay no attention to the *New York Times Magazine* article in 1974 that claimed that Intermountain Aviation "was used to aid in covert CIA operations." Look, that was a long time ago. And Evergreen, unlike SAT, helps other countries. Remember, in 1985, they "donated" a plane to supply humanitarian aid into Ethiopia.

Evergreen is so nice that even SAT was forced to come to their defense when Evergreen lost its U.S. Postal Service

Express Mail contract in 1989. The *Journal of Commerce* report-ed that SAT "protested the decision to the Postal Service" when Air Train Inc. won with a bid that was $7.6 million lower than Evergreen's.

Some busybodies are likely to make much ado out of the fact that Evergreen is privately held, like SAT, according to the *Journal*. And that Chairman Ned Wallace, who resigned in 1990, had been with the Flying Tiger Line Inc.—with its own government connections—for some 23 years.

Just 'cause Evergreen held the airlift duties contract for the U.S. Southern Command at Howard Air Force Base in Panama prior to 1990 does not prove any direct ties to the U.S. nation-al security apparatus. And what do *Aviation Week* and *Space Technology* really know anyway?

All I know is I'm proud to welcome to Columbus an airline that flew Imelda Marcos back to the Philippines in 1991. To think that our very own Rickenbacker Airport would be privi-leged to house the airline that was reported on in the *Washington Post* as follows: "After landing in a chartered Evergreen Airline Boeing 747 with more than 200 supporters and journalists, the former first lady was held up at Manila Airport for more than two hours... Among her entourage were 200 American security men."

We were lucky to get Evergreen to come here in 1992 to handle "freight in the Columbus area primarily for The Limited," as the *Dispatch* reported. Just like we were really unlucky Southern Air Transport came here to fly to Hong Kong for The Limited.

See, SAT: Bad. Evergreen: Good.

We're the luckiest city in the world. We should get down on our knees and thank God, or Limited head Les Wexner, that Evergreen Airlines would lease a plane to "federal investigators...a 747 studded with censors...to re-create the fuel tank temperatures of doomed TWA Flight 800 just before it exploded," according to the *Seattle Times*.

Do you think an airline associated with the CIA would do something that nice?

May 13, 1999

Evergreen Is
Ever Undercover

Thank God we finally got somebody to replace the former Southern Air Transport (SAT) after the company went bankrupt amidst allegations that its pilots and planes were used in CIA drug-running operations.

Evergreen International Airlines began racing "time-sensitive cargo" from Kuala Lumpur to Rickenbacker International Airport at the beginning of August 2001. They're aiding some of our best corporate citizens, "such as The Limited and Eddie Bauer," according to the *Columbus Dispatch*, where no-doubt garments are made in state-of-the-art, cheery facilities by well-paid Third World employees.

I was so excited I took a few minutes to research Evergreen's history. Evergreen, originally based in McMinnville, Oregon, expanded from a small helicopter company in the 1960s "to a major international airline with secret government contracts," according to the Portland, Oregon *Free Press*.

The Oregonian reported that "Evergreen Airline Company, Evergreen International Airlines Inc., was built on remnants of two older airlines—one a wholly owned CIA proprietary, or front company, and the other a virtual branch of the U.S. Forest Service that for years secretly had helped the CIA recruit paramilitary personnel."

In 1975, after a series of embarrassing revelations during Senator Frank Church's investigation of the CIA, the "company" liquidated Intermountain Aviation Inc. of Marana, Arizona, near Tucson. Intermountain's assets were purchased by two Oregon companies that the CIA selected: Evergreen and Rosenbalm Aviation Inc. But Evergreen was the big winner. One of the CIA's top aviation officers, the legendary covert ops expert George Doole, worked for Evergreen as a director. Prior to this, Doole managed all of the CIA's proprietary airlines. The CIA selected Evergreen to take over the agency's airbase at Marana. An investigation by the Pulitzer Prize-winning *Oregonian* documented that "The CIA offered Intermountain's substantial Arizona assets only to Evergreen."

What followed was a decade of privileged treatment and government contracts to the airline. Evergreen purchased the CIA's Arizona assets at a fraction of their real worth. An Arthur Andersen financial statement indicates that Evergreen's assets nearly doubled from $25 million to more than $45 million one year after the deal. Evergreen's revenues rose from $8 million to $10 million range in 1975 to $77.9 million by 1979, according to U.S. Civil Aeronautics Board documents.

In 1984, CBS News reported that the CIA was using a "network of private companies" to fly military weapons to Central America to support the Contra rebels trying to overthrow the Sandinista regime in Nicaragua. CBS named both Southern Air and Evergreen Air as involved in the arms shipments. The day after the broadcast, the *Washington Post* reported, "Private airlines, including Evergreen, were owned by the CIA during the Vietnam War, but the agency has said that the airline has since been sold."

The *New York Times* jumped in a day later with the following lead: "The Central Intelligence Agency is using small private airlines to fly guns and other military supplies to United States-backed forces in Central America, and false flight plans are sometimes filed to cover up the shipments." The *Times* mentioned Evergreen by name.

When Doole died in March 1985, the *Times* reported that Evergreen International Aviation in Marana placed a bronze plaque on the wall acknowledging Doole's more than 20-year service with the CIA. Like Rickenbacker, the huge airfield formerly operated by the CIA was now owned by the county government (Pinal County, Arizona). The plaque noted that Doole was "founder, chief executive officer & board of directors of Air America Inc., Air Asia Company Ltd., Civil Air Transport Company Ltd." Air America's planes were used, according to U.S. intelligence documents, to facilitate the transportation of opium from Laos to U.S. military bases in the Philippines and Thailand during the Vietnam War. The airline's nickname was "Opium Air."

Following the incident when Sandinistas shot down a Southern Air Transport C-123K cargo plane that led to the Iran-Contra arms- and drug-running scandal, the *Washington Post* reported that SAT President William G. Langton had been previously associated with Evergreen International Airlines. The *Oregonian* investigative report came out in 1988 revealing how well Evergreen Airlines was doing. But by 1994, the airline had defaulted on $125 million in junk bonds, according to the *Portland Free Press*.

In 1997, Evergreen was caught up in a huge scandal when scores of former military planes were diverted to covert CIA operations under the guise of "firefighting." The *Free Press* reported that Evergreen International Airlines was involved in the covert activities. Gary Eitel, a decorated Vietnam combat pilot and law-enforcement officer, found employment at

Evergreen and "observed that card-carrying CIA personnel were on Evergreen property acting as Evergreen employees."

When the *Columbus Dispatch* reported on Evergreen's stepped-up presence here, the paper concluded: "Still, Rickenbacker officials are hoping for even more cargo activity, and [Jeff] Clark said Evergreen is in the process of determining whether it will operate additional flights from Columbus to South America."

Columbia may be a good place to start for those "time-sensitive" deliveries, eh?

August 9, 2001

Dark Side Of The Moon

After Texas Governor George W. Bush faltered in New Hampshire in early 2000, a shadowy right-wing network came to his rescue in South Carolina, turning a certain primary defeat into a double-digit victory. As the *Washington Post* noted, "An array of conservative groups have come in to reinforce Bush's message with phone banks, radio ads and mailings of their own."

Washington Post columnist Richard Cohen asserted that "Bush embraces the far-right fringe." From the racists who prohibit interracial dating at Bob Jones University to the moronic Confederate flag wavers, from Rush Limbaugh to Pat Robertson, and from the most extreme elements of the right-to-life movement to the Moonies, the Bush family network prevailed. NBC's Tim Russert pointed out that George W. was now "indebted to Pat Robertson, Jerry Falwell" and the Christian right.

Dutifully, the *Washington Times*—a paper owned by self-proclaimed messiah and cult leader Reverend Sun Myung Moon—ran a headline stating, "Bush scoffs at assertion he moved too far right." The bizarre and almost unbelievable relationship between the Bush family and the 80-year-old Moon is the dirty little secret of George W.'s campaign for President.

To understand the role the Moonies play in U.S. politics, one must start with Ryoichi Sasakawa, identified in a 1992 PBS

Frontline investigative report as a key money source for Reverend Moon's far-flung world empire. In the 1930s, Sasakawa was one of Japan's leading fascists. He organized a private army of 1,500 men equipped with 20 warplanes. His men dressed in black shirts to emulate Mussolini. Sasakawa was an "uncondemned Class-A war criminal" suddenly freed with another accused war criminal—Yoshio Kodama, a leading figure in Japan's organized crime syndicate Yakuza—in 1948.

In January 1995, Japan's KYODO news service uncovered documents establishing that the one-time fascist war criminal suspect was earmarked as an informer by U.S. military intelligence two months prior to his unexplained release. Declassified documents link Kodama's release to the CIA. During World War II, the Kodama Agency, according to U.S. Army counterintelligence records, consisted of "systematically looting China of its raw materials" and dealing in heroin, guns, tungsten, gold, industrial diamonds and radium.

Both Sasakawa and Kodama's CIA ties are a reoccurring theme in their relationship with the Moonies. In 1977, Congressman Donald Fraser launched an investigation into Moon's background. The 444-page Congressional report alleged Moonie involvement with bribery, bank fraud, illegal kickbacks and arms sales. The report revealed that Moon's 20,000-member Unification Church was a creation of Korean Central Intelligence Agency (KCIA) Director Kim Chong Phil as a political tool to influence U.S. foreign policy. The U.S. CIA was the agency primarily responsible for the founding of the KCIA.

The Moon organizations have denied any links with the Korean government or intelligence community.

Moon, who is Korean, and his two Japanese buddies, Sasakawa and Kodama, first joined together in the 1960s to form the Asian People's Anti-Communist League with the aid of KCIA agents, alleged Japanese organized crime money and financial support from Chinese Generalissimo Chiang Kai-Shek. The League concentrated on uniting fascists, right-wing and anti-Communist forces throughout Asia.

In 1964, League funds set up Moon's Freedom Center in the United States. Kodama served as chief advisor to the Moon subsidiary Win Over Communism, an organization that served to protect Moon's South Korean investments. Sasakawa acted as Win Over Communism's chair.

In 1966, the League merged with the anti-Bolshevik Bloc of Nations, another group with strong fascist ties, to form the World Anti-Communist League (WACL). Later, in the 1980s, the retired U.S. Major General John Singlaub emerged as a key player in the Iran-Contra scandal through his chairmanship of the WACL. Singlaub enlisted paramilitary groups, foreign governments and right-wing Americans to support the Contra cause in Nicaragua.

Moon's Freedom Center served as the headquarters for the League in the United States. During the Iran-Contra hearings, the League was described as "a multi-national network of Nazi war criminals, Latin American death squad leaders, North American racists and anti-Semites and fascist politicians from every continent."

Working with the KCIA, Moon made his first trip to the U.S. in 1965 and obtained an audience with former President Dwight D. Eisenhower. Ike, along with former President Harry S Truman, lent their names to the letterhead of the Moon-created Korean Cultural Freedom Foundation. In 1969, Moon and Sasakawa jointly formed the Freedom Leadership Foundation, a pro-Vietnam War organization that lobbied the U.S. government.

In the 1970s, Moon earned notoriety in the Koreagate scandal after female followers of the Unification Church were accused of entertaining and keeping confidential files on several U.S. congressmen who they "lobbied" at a Washington Hilton Hotel suite rented by the Moonies. The U.S. Senate held hearings concerning Moon's "programmatic bribery of U.S. officials, journalists and others as part of an operation by the Korean CIA to influence the course of U.S. foreign policy."

The Fraser report noted that Moon was paid by the KCIA to stage demonstrations at the United Nations and run pro-South Korean propaganda campaigns. The Congressional investigator for the Fraser report said, "We determine that their [Moonies'] primary interest, at least in the U.S. at that time, was not religious at all but was political, it was attempt to gain power, influence and authority."

After Ronald Reagan's presidential victory in 1980, Moon's political influence increased dramatically. Vice President George Bush, a former CIA director, invited Moon as his guest to the Reagan inauguration. Bush and Moon shared unsavory links to South American underworld figures. In 1980, according to the investigatory magazine *IF*, the Moon organization collaborated with a right-wing military coup in Bolivia that established the region's first narco-state.

Moon's credentials soared in conservative circles in 1982 with the inception of the *Washington Times*. Vice President Bush immediately saw the value of building an alliance with the politically powerful Moon organization, an alliance that Moon claims made Bush president. One ex-Moonie's website claims that during the 1988 Bush-Dukakis battle, Reverend Moon threatened his followers that he'd move all of them out of the U.S. if the evil Dukakis won.

Also in 1982, Moon was convicted of income tax evasion

and spent more than a year in jail.

During the Gulf War, the Moonie-sponsored American Freedom Coalition organized "support the troop" rallies. The *Frontline* documentary identified the *Washington Times* as the most costly piece in Moon's propaganda arsenal, with losses estimated as high as $800 million. Still, Sasakawa's virtual monopoly over the Japanese speedboat gambling industry allowed the money to continue flowing to Moon's U.S. coffers.

The Bush-Moonie connection caused considerable controversy in September 1995, when the former president announced he would be spending nearly a week in Japan on behalf of a Moonie front organization, the Women's Federation for World Peace, founded and led by Moon's wife. Bush downplayed accusations of brain-washing and coercion against the Moonies. The *New York Times* noted that Bush's presence "is seen by some as lending the group [Moonies] legitimacy."

Longtime Moonie member S.P. Simonds wrote an editorial for the *Portland Press Herald* noting the Bushes "didn't need the reported million dollars paid by Moon and were well aware of the Church's history."

Bush shared the podium with Moon's wife and addressed a crowd of 50,000 in the Tokyo dome. Bush told the true believers, "Reverend and Mrs. Moon are engaged in the most important activities going on the world today."

The following year Moon bankrolled a series of "family values" conferences from Oakland to Washington, D.C. The *San Francisco Chronicle* reported, "In Washington, Moon opened his checkbook to such Republican Party mainstays as former Presidents Gerald Ford and George Bush, GOP presidential candidate Jack Kemp and Christian Coalition leader Ralph Reed."

Purdue University Professor of Sociology Anson Shupe, a

longtime Moon watcher, said, "The man accused of being the biggest brainwasher in America has moved into mainstream Republican Americana."

Moon claimed at these family values conferences that he was the "only one who knows all the secrets of God." One of them, according to the *Chronicle*, is that "the husband is the owner of his wife's sexual organs and vice versa."

"President Ford, President Bush, who attended the Inaugural World Convention of the Family Federation for World Peace and all you distinguished guests are famous, but there's something that you do not know," the *Chronicle* quoted Moon as saying. "Is there anyone here who dislikes sexual organs?... Until now you may not have thought it virtuous to value the sexual organs, but from now, you must value them."

In November 1996, Bush arrived in Buenos Aires, Argentina, amid controversy over a newly created Spanish-language Moon weekly newspaper called *Tiempos del Mundo*. Bush smoothed things over as the principal speaker at the paper's opening dinner on November 23.

The former president then traveled with Moon to neighboring Uruguay to help him open a Montevideo seminary to train 4,200 young Japanese women to spread the word of the Unification Church across Latin America. The young Japanese seminarians were later accused of laundering $80 million through an Uruguayan bank, according to the *St. Petersburg Times*.

The *Times* also reported that when Reverend Jerry Falwell's university faced bankruptcy, Moon's group bailed it out with millions of dollars in loans and grants.

The *New York Times* noted in 1997 that Moon "has been reaching out to conservative Christians in this country in the last few years by emphasizing shared goals like support for sexual abstinence outside of marriage and opposition to homosexuality." Moon also appeals to the Second Amendment crowd. In March 1999, the *Washington Post* reported that the messiah owned the lucrative Kahr Arms Company through Saeilo Inc.

It's the shadowy network around the Moonies that the elder Bush could have called in to bail out his son's campaign in South Carolina. Make no mistake, George W. of Texas is little more than a frontman for the restoration of his father's unsavory connections, who hide behind the veil of national security to avoid accountability.

February 24, 2000

Moon Over Korea

A controversial religious cult leader and conservative publisher may have directly violated the U.S. trade embargo aimed at containing North Korea's military build up, an independent news website reported. The disclosure of U.S. intelligence documents could prove embarrassing to Republican presidential nominee George W. Bush.

In October 2000, Consortiumnews.com published U.S. Defense Intelligence Agency (DIA) documents disclosing that Unification Church leader Reverend Sun Myung Moon's business empire funneled millions of dollars in secret payments to North Korean Communist leaders during the early 1990s. At the time, North Korea was in desperate need of hard currency to advance its nuclear weapons program.

The DIA documents reveal that Moon surreptitiously traveled to North Korea "between 30NOV91 and 07DEC91" and "made donations to KN [North Korea] of 450 billion yen [$3.5 billion] in 1991 and $3 million in 1993." The $3 million, according to the documents, was a birthday present to the country's Communist dictator Kim Jong II.

Moon, a native South Korean, is a resident alien of the U.S. and subject to U.S. law.

"In January '94, a Japanese trading company 'Touen Shoji' in Suginami-Ku, Tokyo, purchased 12 F- and G-class submarines from the Russian Pacific Fleet headquarters. These submarines were then sold to a KN trading company. Although this transaction garnered a great deal of coverage in the Japanese press, it was not disclosed at the time that Touen Shoji is an affiliate of the Unification Church," a DIA document reads.

The Bush family, particularly former President George Bush, has had long-standing political and financial ties to Reverend Moon, the self-proclaimed second coming of Christ.

In a Consortiumnews.com four-part series, one of the United States' foremost investigative reporters, Robert Parry, who broke many of the Iran-Contra stories in the 1980s for the Associated Press and *Newsweek*, outlines the connections between the Bush family and Moon. After he left office in January 1993, the former president received hefty payments from Moon, reported in the seven-figure range, for speeches and other personal services. Parry reports a former "well-placed" Unification Church leader as saying that "$10 million" was earmarked for former President Bush.

During the 2000 presidential election, the Moon-owned *Washington Times* championed the Republican candidacy of George W. Bush and mounted harsh attacks against Democratic candidate Al Gore. In December 1999, the *Washington Times* accused Gore of being "delusional" and called the vice president "a politician who not only manufactures gross, obvious lies about himself and his achievements but appears to actually believe these confabulations."

Gore's supposed "delusions" emerged as a key, and successful, attack theme, taking on a life of their own. Many voters now believe that Gore claimed to have "invented" the Internet. What Gore actually said was, "During my service in the United States Congress, I took the initiative in creating the Internet." Two actual Internet "inventors," Vinton Cerf and Robert Kahn, have vigorously defended Gore as the key politician in Washington who took the "initiative" to support the Internet in its infancy.

In 1988, when Republican presidential nominee George Bush was trailing significantly in the polls, the *Washington Times* printed an unconfirmed rumor that Democratic presidential nominee Michael Dukakis had undergone psychiatric treatment.

Moon was convicted of income tax evasion in 1982 and spent more than a year in jail. That same year, he founded the *Washington Times*. Moon also owns the *World and I* journal, *Insight* magazine and earlier this year he purchased the UPI wire service. When the *Washington Times* appointed Wesley Pruden editor-in-chief in 1991, President Bush invited the new editor to a private White House lunch "just to tell you how valuable the *Times* has become in Washington, where we read it every day," the *Washington Times* reported.

The *Times* proved to be one of President Bush's staunchest defenders, launching several attacks against Iran-Contra special prosecutor Lawrence Walsh during his investigation of Bush and high-ranking officials in his administration. During the '92 campaign, the *Times* raised questions about Clinton's alleged ties to Communism, even suggesting the Rhodes scholar may have been recruited by the KGB during a college trip to Moscow. The *Times* is the paper most responsible for breaking news on the so-called Whitewater scandal and the Lewinsky affair.

Ironically, Moon's newspaper has repeatedly attacked the Clinton-Gore administration for being soft on North Korea. As Parry puts it: "Moon helped deliver the means for the Communist state to advance exactly the strategic threat that Moon's newspaper now says will require billions of U.S. tax dollars to thwart."

October 19, 2000

Dubya's Full Moon Rising

The Reverend Sun Myung Moon continued his lunacy this spring with another mass wedding—this time in Midtown Manhattan, where he hitched Catholic Archbishop Emmanuel Milango to a Korean acupuncturist. But that's just the sideshow.

The *Christian Science Monitor* provided a much better look at Moon's recent public prominence under Bush the Younger's administration. Last fall, Moon raised his profile by joining with Louis Farrakhan of the Nation of Islam to co-sponsor the Million Family March in Washington. In April, the eightysomething Moon completed a 52-city tour in 52 days dedicated to "strengthening family values in America." Does the rhetoric sound familiar? The tour drew "backers ranging from a former director of Operation Push to a founding member of the Christian Coalition…[and] as many a 3,000 local ministers, politicians and church members to some venues," the *Monitor* reported.

A Moon-sponsored AIDS/HIV school curriculum centered around abstinence has been adopted by a few schools. Perhaps they should adopt a political science curriculum that requires students to read the 1978 Congressional report on "Koreagate," which linked Moon's Unification Church to covert operations of the Korean Central Intelligence Agency.

Moon, an ardent foe of democracy and pitchman for a worldwide theology, controls both the *Washington Times* and United Press International, along with dozens of other newspapers and magazines. News reports place Moon's subsidy to the money-losing *Washington Times* at $100 million a year. Not too high a price for Ronald Reagan's "favorite" newspaper and the Bush family's biggest political promoter.

Of course, the Bushes and Moons have covert activities in common, with Bush Sr. as former CIA director and longtime Moon associate Kim Jong Pil working for the South Korean CIA and assisting the Unification Church's influence-building in both the U.S. and Japan.

Moon's gospel is that humans are the children of Satan because the serpent seduced Eve in the Garden. The only way people can find their "true lineage with God" is through Moon and his wife—"the true parents."

The *Monitor* quotes Moon at a New Hampshire speech: "If a woman deliberately avoids having children, she is a substandard animal." He has also suggested that American women are descended from a "line of prostitutes."

Ironically, one of Moon's key early backers was Ryoichi Sasakawa, a leading figure in Japan's Yakuza organized crime family, according to the definitive tome *Yakuza* by David E. Kaplan and Alec Dubro. Maybe Sasakawa tutored Moon on the prostitution racket, making the self-proclaimed Messiah an expert.

In January 1995, Moon's Women's Federation for World Peace, the group that paid Bush Sr. at least a million dollars for a speech, also bailed out Jerry Falwell's debt-ridden Liberty University. According to IRS documents, the Moon front funneled $3.5 million through an "educational grant" to the

Christian Heritage Foundation, which in turn bought up a big chunk of Liberty's debt.

Critics have long charged that Moon is systematically buying well-known religious, cultural and political figures with his mysterious sources of money. His agenda is not hidden—a worldwide theocracy where he and his wife reign. Moon openly declares, in speeches to his followers, that his goal is "the natural subjugation of the U.S. and its people under theocratic rule."

Bush Sr. called Moon "the man with the vision." Through his ubiquitous front groups, with innocuous names like the American Freedom Coalition, the cult leader is using his ties and influence with the new Bush administration for a last-gasp attempt to align the forces of a new American fascism.

From the outset, it was clear that Shrub would continue repaying the support first granted to Bush the Elder. According to the *Boston Globe*, Moon's *Washington Times* won a reserved front-row seat between the prized stations of Reuters and the *New York Times* in the press room at Bush-Cheney transition headquarters. "The warm reception for the *Washington Times*... surprised even its staff at the first press briefing at the Bush-Cheney headquarters," the *Globe* reported.

If you're interested in reading about the Messiah and his actual family values, the memoir of ex-daughter-in-law Nansook Hong, *In the Shadow of the Moons*, is a good starting point. She portrays the "true family" and their kids as spoiled brats doted on hand and foot by brainwashed American cult members.

Hong writes: "No one knows the pain of a straying husband like True Mother, she [Mrs. Moon] assured me. I was stunned. We had all heard rumors for years about Sun Myung Moon's affairs and the children he sired out of wedlock, but here was

True Mother confirming the truth of these stories."

"What Father did was in God's plan," Hong explained. Apparently it's also God's plan for Reverend Moon to own Kahr Arms, which recently acquired Auto-Ordnance Corp, maker of the legendary "Tommy gun."

After all, Jesus owes Moon a lot. Just ask the reverend. Since, according to Moon's theology, only married individuals can enter the kingdom of heaven, Moon had to match Jesus up with an "elderly Korean woman" retroactively in order to get Christ in to see God the Father, Hong tells us. Not as hard to get the hook-up with Bush the Father and his Only Befuddled Son.

June 7, 2001

Impeach Bush

The *Columbus Free Press* is launching its own Office of Total Counter-Information Awareness. In the last few months, we've accumulated enough information to warrant the impeachment of President George Bush.

First, let's recall Bush's strange relationship with that bizarre little company in Lansing, Michigan, known as Bioport. The company, despite failing various FDA inspections and being accused of bad record-keeping, holds the only federal contract for producing the anthrax vaccine. Bush has rewarded Bioport with favors such as ongoing military protection, and within weeks of 9/11 granted them a contract that tripled the price per vaccine. Now, add into the mix that the Strangelovian, CIA-connected Battelle and Britain's top-secret Porton Down labs are partners with Bioport.

Owners and investors in Bioport include former Chairman of Joint Chiefs of Staff William Crowe and Fuad El-Hibri. Public records and foreign press reports have linked El-Hibri to the selling of anthrax to Saudi Arabia after the Pentagon refused to. He's also a business associate of the bin Laden family. A real Congressional investigation of Bush's relationships with the bin Laden family, El-Hibri and the related drug bank BCCI would easily lead to the President's impeachment.

Second, the President's utter contempt for U.S. citizens was displayed in his appointments of three criminals: the pompous pipe-puffing Admiral John Poindexter, Elliott Abrams of Iran-Contra infamy and wanted war criminal Henry Kissinger.

Poindexter, who now runs the Office of Total Information Awareness, is busily keeping files on every U.S. citizen. Well, put this in your file on Poindexter: He supervised the illegal arms for hostage sale to Iran that violated the Arms Export Control Act; he sanctioned the funneling of profits from that illegal sale into the Nicaraguan Contras, a group more famous for its drug-running than fighting the Sandinistas; he lied about his activities and destroyed evidence during the Congressional investigation; and a federal jury found him guilty of lying and obstructing justice. But the fix was apparently in and two conservative federal judges overturned his conviction.

After lying to Congress about the Iran-Contra scandal and being convicted on two counts, Abrams was pardoned by Bush Sr. Now thanks to Bush Jr., he's the top Middle East advisor on the National Security Council.

And what can we say about Kissinger? From the "secret bombings" of Cambodia to the overthrow of Chile's democracy, there's perhaps no figure more hated in the world than the good doctor. This didn't stop Junior from appointing him to cover up the real causes of 9/11. Fortunately Special K was forced to resign when he refused to disclose his clients from his private "consulting firm" Kissinger and Associates. We would have stood a better chance of getting to the truth of 9/11 had we dug up the bones of Earl Warren and created another bogus Warren Commission.

Meanwhile, the forces of Big Oil surrounding Bush are hell-bent on stealing the Iraqi people's petroleum. Somehow they seem able to convince the U.S. people that Baby Jesus himself put that oil in Iraq for us to pilfer in the name of God and country.

Despite the Bush Jr. administration's best efforts to hide the crucial role of Bush Sr. in arming Iraq with biochemical weapons in the 1980s—including Secretary of State Colin Powell's bullying the U.N. into allowing him to remove 8,000 key pages of Iraq's 12,000-page dossier on weapons—the story continues to break.

Finally, Bush's foreign policy contains the rabid elements of inbred elitist ignorance. A week before Christmas, Human Rights Watch reported that the U.S. military violated international law in Afghanistan by indiscriminately dropping cluster bombs in civilian areas. That same week, the Bush administration announced a new strategy of covert actions and pre-emptive strikes, including nukes, against any country that dares attack U.S. troops now stationed in at least 148 nations throughout the world. The President announced his new version of Star Wars Jr., guaranteeing huge profits for the U.S. military-industrial complex and ensuring we will continue to be the nation with the greatest stockpile of weapons of mass destruction.

For these and other reasons too numerous to reveal, the President must be impeached.

Columbus Free Press
January 2003

The Banality Of Evil

The Cold War techno-whizzes at Battelle are having a hard time going "green" in the New World Order. What started out as a seemingly innocuous request to renew a hazardous waste permit has erupted into a full-blown neighborhood war.

Battelle's attempt to bring its facilities into compliance with government environmental regulations has pried open the door to the Dr. Strangelove Institute. What is revealed from a quick peek inside is an institution "out of control." A recent leak of an internal audit shows Battelle to have two types of problems: some systemic and some just stupid. The stupidity seems bred of a combination of arrogance and casualness. Sources inside Battelle confirmed these *Free Press* suspicions.

What is certain is that more "shocking" information about the Columbus-based Battelle will emerge as they morph from weapons wizards to environmental techno-fixers.

It's not the renewal of Battelle's application that would allow it to continue to store up to 500 gallons of hazardous waste at 505 King Ave. that started the war. Rather, it's the "modification" to store up to 9,625 gallons of hazardous and radioactive waste that led the neighbors to request an "information session" with the Ohio EPA and the U.S. EPA on December 5.

The meeting held at the Fifth Avenue Elementary School

started out combatively. After Tim Wagner of the Battelle Permit Opposition Committee was allowed to ask two questions, Miles Davidson of the Ohio EPA read a letter from Cleve Ricksecker, president of the Short North Business Association. Ricksecker's letter initially stunned the audience before leading to near open rebellion: "Who among us does not have hazardous waste stored at their house, including gasoline, paint thinner and weed killer?" Ricksecker asked.

Ricksecker asserted, "That every car that travels on Fifth Avenue poses a bigger risk" than the uranium 235, 238, cobalt 60 and various other radioactive isotopes stored at Battelle. He stated, without documentation that, "Battelle has an excellent safety record."

Amid the chaotic responses to the Ricksecker letter came a woman's voice with the most cogent and pertinent question: "Did Battelle make a contribution to this holiday thing going on tonight, which is the reason Cleve isn't here?" Like the vast majority of key questions asked on December 5, there was no answer from the Battelle or government representatives.

Kenneth Brog, a vice president at Battelle, tried to calm the crowd by saying, "We're cleaning up all of our facilities in which we have done nuclear materials work for the Department of Energy [DOE] and the Nuclear Regulatory Commission [NEC] for the past 50 years." Battelle, applying for DOE dollars, has estimated over $100 million in radioactive clean-up costs at their facilities.

Thus, according to Brog, it's Battelle's own estimates and hunger for government clean-up subsidies that caused it to be placed on *U.S. News and World Report's* list of the Dirty Dozen radioactive polluters in the U.S.

Brog explained that the expanded storage capacity was needed as "part of the Battelle-Columbus Lab Decommissioning

Project—which is the clean-up of our sites for the work we've done for the DOE and the NRC since 1943, dating back to the Manhattan Project."

Delivered in Brog's monotone and scientific jargon, such revelations slipped past most of the crowd unnoticed. Coupled with the bureaucratese of the government officials, the language underscored Hannah Arendt's famous assessment of the Nazi Adolf Eichmann—Battelle is a Cold War monument to "the banality of evil."

Brog, like Ricksecker, claimed that Battelle had an "outstanding environmental, safety and health record."

Ed Lim of the Ohio EPA, known in environmental circles as "Mr. WTI" for being instrumental in bringing the nation's largest hazardous waste incinerator on line in East Liverpool, Ohio, explained that as long as Battelle is in compliance they would automatically receive their renewal and, in all probability, the modification. The Ohio EPA is dependent on Battelle for the self-reporting paperwork that constitutes compliance.

Tom Meyer of the Battelle Permit Opposition Committee promised to show a record of "non-compliance" with safety and environmental standards at Battelle. "This is a profit-making venture for Battelle. They're making big money off this deal," Meyer said.

Meyer proved true to his word when, on December 13, the Battelle Permit Opposition Committee made public a leaked internal audit of a "Battelle Safety and Health Survey" conducted by independent consultants at Battelle's request. Richard Sahli, director of the Ohio Environmental Council, charged that the "contents are shocking."

"Many of the violations are fundamental in nature and demonstrate that Battelle doesn't have even the basic elements in place for managing its waste safely," said Sahli.

Wagner found the findings "frightening" and claimed "the audit clearly shows a facility out of control."

Sahli, formerly the Ohio EPA's chief legal counsel, challenged the public and reporters to read the audit carefully: "I've successfully prosecuted companies with much better records than Battelle."

The systemic problems are obvious in the audit: lack of training for staff and supervisory personnel on how to handle radioactive waste; no one assigned to supervisory authority for overseeing the development and implementation of a health and safety plan; no quality control program in place; no ability to document whether its facilities exceed the amount of radioactive material it is legally allowed to have on site; no system to monitor on-site radioactive materials; no ability to identify and retrieve radioactive materials in the event of an emergency; and no ability to determine where Battelle's radioactive materials have been disposed.

Perhaps even more shocking are Battelle's documented violations of worker safety standards. Brog and Ricksecker aside, various comments from the audit speak volumes as to Battelle's verified environmental and safety practices:

DESCRIPTION OF FINDING: "Door not posted. A contaminated microwave oven in this lab is untagged." ACTION REQUIRED: "Post hallway door. Survey microwave for radioactive activity—tag NO FOOD USE."

DESCRIPTION OF FINDING: "In refrigerator radioactive labeled liquid phase materials being stored in glass. Door not posted. Radioactive samples (may be waste) being stored on bench top. Contaminated motorized back saw untagged."

ACTION REQUIRED: "Glass containers should be in plastic container. Post door. Provide secure storage for radioactive samples. Tag and survey (smear test)."

DESCRIPTION OF FINDING: "1. Dosing hoods in use are unfiltered. 2. The vent to interior air of building. Such hoods are used to inject or otherwise apply radioactive materials* to test animals. *such as I-131 and C-14."

ACTION REQUIRED: "Refit hood with filter or vent to charcoal filter or scrubber."

DESCRIPTION OF FINDING: "Rad trash overflowing. Rad work surface not properly covered (near sink)."

ACTION REQUIRED: "Pick up trash. Re-cover surface."

DESCRIPTION OF FINDING: "C-14 has been used in this lab. 1. No padlocks on the refrigerator. 2. Solvent smell (C-14 labeled?) from the refrigerator when opened. 3. Laboratory very untidy. 4. Laboratory is unoccupied currently but unlocked with sources in the refrigerator."

ACTION REQUIRED: "1. Put padlocks on the refrigerator. 2. Check refrigerator for surface contamination and clean. 3. Clean lab generally after survey for surface contamination. 4. Lock lab door when unoccupied."

In all, the independent auditors documented 193 deficiencies at Battelle with 92 of them falling into specific unsafe working condition deficiencies.

Battelle managed to correct 52 of these 92 deficiencies within one day. These fall into the category of errors caused by stupidity and neglect. Most of their systemic problems remain unchanged.

In response to the audit report, the *Free Press* spoke with one current and one former Battelle employee. Neither would speak for attribution.

The *Free Press* was able to verify that the former employee who claimed to have "a Q-clearance that will get me to the fifth floor of the Pentagon" had worked at Battelle and had undergone rad waste training. "OSU's a worse offender. Far worse than Battelle could ever be," said the former employee.

This theme—that Ohio State University, located right on the other side of King Avenue, is the real offender—also came up the December 7 Battelle Permit Opposition Committee meeting. Pete Strimer, who met with Battelle officials, reported that they claimed Battelle "pales by comparison to the Arthur James Cancer Center at OSU."

"Nobody looks across the street. Battelle at least tries to follow regulations. Nobody looks at OSU," the ex-employee said. "I delivered a sealed source to OSU with a radioactive satellite component and the graduate student opened it up right in front of me and asked: 'What's this?' At the Cancer Center they're pitching low-level radioactive waste into the trash,".

The former rad waste worker said, "It's not Battelle's fault that the security guards don't follow procedures. You put a yellow or magenta tape on the door and that means "Stay out!' But they say 'Screw this' and go in anyway. If they're stupid enough to heat their coffee up in a radioactive contaminated building it's their fault. If the whole building's hot, like buildings two and three, you shouldn't have to post every room and microwave."

A current Battelle employee differs in this assessment: "A lot of those security guards look awfully young, like college kids. I'm not sure they understand what they're doing. They're just so casual."

"Look, some of that stuff has been locked up in a room for 50 years. There's no record of the original source—it was all top secret and you can't just move it," explained the ex-employee. "In the old days, people were very casual about radioactive material. In the '50s and '60s the scientists would just take whatever they wanted and not have to account for it because they were working on top-secret projects. Those blue badges didn't have to account for anything."

The current Battelle employee confirmed, "It's not just the blue badges. You've got the higher orange badges and the invisible stripes. For years, just your connection with certain levels of the DOD [Department of Defense] and DOE meant that nobody hassled you. In building number three they've had to scrape off inches of concrete, but they don't tell us anything. All I know is what I read in the papers."

At the December 5 public hearing, Brog stated unequivocally that Battelle was not "incinerating radioactive waste."

On July 15, 1992, the independent auditors witnessed the burning of animal carcasses with a "carbon-14 burden." They noted that "no stack monitoring for radiation was conducted during the burn." Battelle's own permit review records reveal that "no additional emission control equipment is associated with this [incineration] unit." No fly ash screen, no scrubbers, no nothing. The incinerator's shadow reflects on the Olentangy River. And the newly proposed radioactive and hazardous waste facility will sit on the banks of a 100-year floodplain. The carbon-14 bottom ash is collected and disposed of at the Franklin County landfill.

Brog has clarified his earlier unequivocal statement: Yes, they burned the animal carcasses, but the carbon-14 was of such a low dose that they didn't have to notify the EPA. Once again, no documentation was provided for this claim.

As the *Free Press* went to press with this story, an anonymous source contacted the paper to help put things in perspective: "You shouldn't worry about that nerve gas. It's stored out at West Jefferson."

Donna Sheehan, writing recently in *Everyone's Backyard*, offers the following advice to those organizing against hazardous and radioactive waste: "Looking back, I see that all of the tactics we used to stop the spraying, the only ones that worked were civil disobedience and legal action. When anti-toxin groups call for advice, I tell them not to waste time pleading, negotiating and lobbying. My advice to them is, 'Block the spray trucks and take them to court. And don't wait, do it now!'"

Columbus Free Press
January 1994

Battelle's Hot Pond

According to sources inside the Battelle Columbus Institute, the pond at Battelle's West Jefferson facility is contaminated with radioactive waste. A hazardous waste removal specialist currently employed at Battelle told the *Free Press*, "I probably shouldn't be telling you this, but I've seen people playing and fishing in that lake—it's definitely hot."

Another employee in hazardous waste confirmed that "the scientist originally in charge of that site let things get out of control and the tried to cover up the extent of the contamination."

Both employees work for the recently created Battelle Columbus Institute Decommissioning Project (BCIDP) under the supervision of Kenneth Brog, a vice president at Battelle. The picture painted by these two Battelle employees is one that pits the BCIDP against the Battelle Columbus Institite (BCI).

Essentially, the BCIDP is responsible for bringing the Battelle facilities into compliance with current EPA standards. "Battelle has been dragging its feet for years on this cleanup," said a waste removal specialist. "It's a blue collar versus white collar battle—the scientists with BCI don't like the hazardous waste technicians telling them what to do."

The atmosphere at Battelle, according to both employees, is hostile and tense following the leak of an internal Battelle audit that documented 193 "deficiencies" in hazardous and radioactive waste handling at the Institute.

"The person that leaked that audit is gone, they're fired," said one source. The other source claims that a female friend was fired approximately a year ago for pushing Battelle to correct the problems in the audit.

Additionally, two anonymous letters were sent to Richard Sahli, director of the Ohio Environmental Council, after the initial audit was leaked. The letters, written in different typeface, are remarkably similar in style and may have been written by the same person. The letters point out that up until last year, the head of Custodial Services at Battelle was also in charge of hazardous and radioactive waste clean-up.

The hazardous waste specialist who spoke with the Free Press also supplied a hand-drawn map of the West Jefferson site. According to the map, there are four key buildings close to the lake: the Battelle buildings are coded as BN1, BN2, BN3 and BN4 ("BN" stands for Battelle North). Building BN3 is the decommissioned nuclear research reactor most likely responsible for the radioactive contamination of the pond.

Building BN4, several sources say, is the site under heavy military guard that contains who-knows-what from the glory days of biological and chemical warfare agents. Two current employees assert that nerve gas is stored here.

"Don't get me wrong, we're working hard to try and bring Battelle into compliance," said a hazardous waste specialist. "It's just that there's so much resistance from the scientists in the front office, and things are much better than they were two years ago."

Another employee reports that in the initial inventory for the BCIDP, "You would find strange stuff." For example, he said in a file cabinet in an office, two uranium ore samples were just sitting in a box.

"It's tough getting these blue badges [scientists] to change…

It's hard to get them to take radioactive contamination seriously. They're simply contemptuous of all us tech workers," one source concluded.

Kenneth Brog, a Battelle vice president in charge of the Decommissioning Project, was "not available" to speak to the *Free Press*.

Columbus Free Press
February 1994

Scrap Metal Meltdown

Allen Hogan's 27-acre scrap yard, the Autojumble, and his adjacent house stand on Mansfield's Fifth Avenue as a radioactive testament to the Cold War. Just exactly how Hogan and his young daughter Erin became two of the last casualties of the nuclear arms race is a reminder that the U.S. military-industrial complex's fear of the former Soviet Union may still be responsible, to borrow a military term, for collateral damages.

On a cold, March day in 1994, Allen Hogan drove to a Columbus auction and bid on Lot 178 offered by the U.S. Defense Revitalization and Marketing Office (DRMO). In an apparent bargain, Hogan bought 2,180 pounds of scrap magnesium for $75, to resell.

"I looked at the math," he said. Hogan figured the magnesium was worth $400 to $500. "It looked like a no-brainer."

What the government failed to disclose at the sale, but now readily admits, is that Hogan unknowingly took possession of hot waste from a former Minuteman nuclear missile, made up of a radioactive magnesium-thorium alloy. Hogan had his ton of "scrap magnesium" trucked to his Mansfield salvage yard. For nearly three years, Allen worked and Erin played, and the little girl helped her dad sort through the scrap metal, surrounded by high levels of radiation.

"The stuff got drug around and kicked and stomped and

spread and shoved around and stuck in various corners," Hogan said. He didn't have a clue the material might be contaminated.

Hogan recalls that he and Erin would gather trash on their property and burn it in a barrel during those three years. Government records indicate that in a later cleanup, a radiation-contaminated burn barrel was removed from the Autojumble. Eventually, the nuclear waste contaminated virtually the entire property.

Hogan's medical records indicate that in January and April of 1995, he was examined for nasal inflammation, tender sinuses and a nasal septum defect, all likely symptoms from breathing radioactive material. He couldn't go to Christmas dinners at the in-laws the year of his nasal problems. "I laid home on Christmas day because I couldn't breathe," he recalled.

In October 1996, amidst growing health problems, Hogan contracted with Northern Ohio Scrap Service of Cleveland to crush and remove various car bodies. The scrap service took the junk cars to the Luntz Corporation in Canton for shredding and recycling.

In November 1996, Lake County Auto Recyclers of Perry, a subcontractor, returned four crushed cars to the Autojumble after the cars had set off a "radioactive antenna" at the Luntz Corporation. Hogan determined that what the four cars had in common was the scrap magnesium he had stored in their trunks. In a later affidavit, he said, "It occurred to me that there might be a connection."

Within days, Hogan contacted DRMO in hopes of confirming his suspicion. Ben Wilmouth soon called from the Radiation Safety Office at Wright-Patterson Air Force Base and set up a mid-December meeting. Wilmouth came out, photographed and surveyed the property, and told Hogan that it was probably "mag-thor" radioactive waste.

Hogan contends in a lawsuit filed in December 1999 in U.S. District Court in Columbus that Wilmouth assured him "that the government would take whatever steps necessary to take care of the situation, and that they would remove the mag-thor from my property." Naively, Hogan took the government at its word and assumed "that would be the end of the problem."

Several U.S. Air Force personnel descended on the Autojumble in January 1997. Their mission was to remove the mag-thor scrap. Hogan claims that they told him the mag-thor "was nothing to worry about." At the end of January, Wilmouth returned with still more personnel to haul out the four radioactive cars and a flatbed truck full of mag-thor. It appeared all was going well.

In April 1997, Wilmouth returned again, to arrange the "big, final cleanup" that would solve the problem. Hogan says that Wilmouth and other government officials repeatedly reassured him that there was nothing to worry about and everything would be as good as new.

Hogan swears that he "told the officials that we had handled, slept near, worked and played in these radioactive materials, and even burned pieces of it for years. They advised me there was no problem."

On June 10, 1997, the government installed a project office trailer on Hogan's property to coordinate the crew of up to 16 workers who toiled for three-and-a-half weeks on site. Air Force representatives promised complete removal of soil if necessary and issued a press release to that effect.

The *Mansfield News Journal* ran an article on the day the cleanup started under the headline, "Radioactive material found: Air Force mistakenly sold scrap material, assisting with cleanup." The story quoted Larry Glidewell, an environmental public affairs specialist with Wright-Patterson Air Force Base, assuring everyone that "most of the 87 pounds of metal was cleared away in January."

"If any soil is shown to contain thorium, it will be removed," Glidewell told the *News Journal*.

The amount of metal Glidewell cited apparently referred to the thorium the government removed. Hogan repeatedly tried to find out how much of the total metal was removed—he bought one ton of "magnesium," not 87 pounds—but received no answers, he said. Glidewell declined to comment for this story, citing government policy on pending litigation, as did other military personnel contacted by *Columbus Alive*.

Air Force officials attempted to clean the property using bulldozers and other heavy equipment in June 1997, but Hogan says, "I continued to find pieces of the mag-thor alloy routinely." After the "big cleanup," Wilmouth came back and took away the additional radioactive material collected by Hogan.

Columbus Alive has viewed a videotape of Wilmouth and Hogan wandering around the Autojumble with Wilmouth's Geiger counter repeatedly registering "hot" for high radiation. Despite these readings, the U.S. Air Force informed Hogan on July 15, 1997, that the U.S. Air Force Office of the Command Surgeon had determined that potential adverse health effects due to the radioactive contamination was "infinitely small to insignificant."

The government paid a third-party contractor to perform a radiological survey of the site and collect soil samples in July 1997. The contractor concluded that no soil excavation was needed. A September 5 letter from the Air Force informed Hogan that both the third party contractor and the government now believed that future health risks to the Hogans were "negligible."

Later in 1997, Hogan bought an old ambulance and stored it for resale. Ironically, he found a booklet in the ambulance giving instructions for the handling of radioactive materials. The book indicated that burning thorium was hazardous to anyone within 1,000 feet.

"My daughter and I had burned pieces of mag-thor alloy as we cleaned parts of the yard. This was the first time I ever had an inkling that there were health risks associated with our exposure to this mag-thor," Hogan recalled. "You're not supposed to be smoking this, ingesting this, putting it on your food. Well, when you're a six-year-old child, where do you put your hands? That's my fear—this is my only child."

Government documents show that another 18 pounds of radioactive waste was removed from the site in October 1998. In February 1999, another 30 pounds of radioactive material was carted away.

Under the Federal Torts Claim Act, Hogan had to file an administrative claim with the Air Force before he could sue for damages. On January 28, 1999, he filed his initial administrative claim alleging permanent injury to his business, property and himself due to the radioactive contamination of his land. He listed himself as the "claimant" but discussed in detail his daughter Erin's exposure to the radioactive waste. Hogan filed a second administrative claim with the Air Force on April 9 alleging that the radioactive contamination of his property constituted an "on-going tort, a continuing nuisance."

The government's response in a June 21, 1999, letter shocked Hogan. Judith M. Regan, chief of the Air Force's Environmental Torts Branch, wrote Hogan that: "We regret that you were sold the magnesium-thorium alloy. However, you have failed to file a timely and substantiated claim. Therefore, we cannot make any payment to you."

Regan reasoned, "Clearly, you suspected the material you had was radioactive in October 1996 when the vehicles you tried to sell were returned to you. You were certainly aware of the radioactive material in December 1996 when an Air Force representative visited your salvage yard. Consequently, any claim you had as a result of the purchase of the magnesium-thorium alloy had to be filed prior to January 1999. However, your first claim was not filed until January 28, 1999, therefore the statute of limitations bars certain aspects of your claim."

Also, since Hogan had not officially listed Erin as a claimant, but merely discussed her, she was also barred from receiving money for her exposure to radiation.

By Regan's reasoning, "If you burned the alloy prior to January 1997, then any claim for injuries is barred by the statute of limitations. If, on the other hand, you burned the alloy in or after January 1997 then your claim is barred by your own negligence, since you knew or should have known you were burning radioactive material. A reasonable person would restrain from burning such material as it might be harmful to do so. Additionally, we believe that any open burning of material you knew to be radioactive would have violated Ohio law."

Hogan is worried the government might actually come after him for violating state law against burning material he didn't know was radioactive. Frustrated with a situation that's escalated to a "slow-moving version of *60 Minutes*," Hogan took a sample of his radioactive junk and left it in an envelope outside the office of a claims lawyer at Wright-Patterson. "I was returning lost property—is that crime?" Hogan asked.

Apparently so, said Hogan. He's been banned from Wright-Patterson and said U.S. attorneys have been waving the incident "like a carrot" in front of his legal counsel.

Eight government attorneys submitted a motion to dismiss Hogan's claims in April 2000. The United States of America, the official plaintiff in the suit, will be arguing its motion before U.S. District Judge James Graham in Columbus in September 2000. The government will argue that Hogan's claim should be dismissed not because it is invalid, but because he should have filed it sooner. For example, since Hogan "remembered suffering from a deviated septum and rectal bleeding in 1994 or 1995," court documents note, he apparently should have surmised then that the government had accidentally contaminated him with radioactive material.

Hogan's attorney James McNamara calls the government's position "absurd." As McNamara sees it, "The government made a huge mistake. They admit they erroneously sold radioactive waste to my client, contaminated his property, assured him that everything would be OK and now they're saying that because he trusted their assurances, he's barred because of a statute of limitation claim."

The 48-year-old father said he's merely seeking retribution for the government's radioactive screw-up. "This is my only hope," Hogan said of the lawsuit. "I thought the Air Force was supposed to protect us from nuclear attacks."

"The bottom line is [the radioactive mag-thor] is not mine. It's theirs," Hogan continued. "They have failed to clean up. They have lied about the health issues. What else is there? I could run away and hide. I could walk away from this, but this is my life's work."

Co-written with Jamie Pietras
September 14, 2000

Toxic Child's Play

Ohio Citizen Action organized scores of local activists to join with parents and children from Marion's contaminated River Valley Middle and High School in a vigil at the Governor's Mansion on August 21, 2000. The candlelight vigil was a desperate plea to Governor Bob Taft to halt the opening of the River Valley Schools and to reassign the students before the beginning of classes.

Demonstrators carried signs asking, "What if they were your kids?" and insisting, "Kids shouldn't play on toxic waste."

The two River Valley schools were built on the site of the former U.S. Army Marion Engineering Depot, the largest facility of its kind in the nation until its closing and subsequent sale to the school district in 1961. The U.S. Army acknowledges dumping, burning and burying solvents, fuel oil, chemical agents and paint on the property for nearly two decades.

Some 70 different chemicals have been documented on or near the school property, including arsenic, vinyl chlorine, tricholoroethyline, benzo (a) pyrene, chromium, lead, PCBs and a host of toxic solvents.

In 1997, the River Valley school nurse reported to the Ohio Department of Health that a disproportionate number of leukemia cases had struck River Valley students and graduates. Between 1966 and 1995, leukemia death rates rose by 122 percent in the city of Marion, and brain cancer death rates increased by 40 percent in the county. The rate of esophageal cancer is 10 times higher than expected, according to Ohio Citizen Action. In 1999, the U.S. Army found "an eminent threat to human health" on Army Reserve property near the schools.

Citizen Action spokesperson Noreen Warnock told those gathered at the vigil that a "state of emergency" exists in Marion, and produced an executive order her organization drafted for the governor's signature. The order calls for "the reassignment of all students to other schools."

Marion resident Mike Griffith shares that sentiment. He told *Columbus Alive*, "All the state and federal pronouncements are always qualified. They'll say there's no eminent or immediate danger but they don't want to assess the combined risk of a hundred chemicals and 20 metals in the soil and air in and around the school."

Kent Krumanaker of Marion suggests that it would be easy to reassign the schoolkids to four other schools in the county. "We wanted it closed three years ago. We need to take these kids out of harm's way," he said.

Last year, River Valley School Superintendent Thomas G. Shade filed an application with the Ohio Schools Facilities Commission Extreme Environmental Contamination Program in order to get funds to build a new school. The application noted that "extensive ongoing investigations by the [Army] Corps have revealed that the entire site is contaminated and it includes a six-acre chemical waste disposal pit."

"Arial photos suggest that former disposal areas may extend below the current middle school building," the application continues. "Surface soil contamination contains unacceptable levels of carcinogenics" which the students are being exposed to through "inhalation, ingestion and dermal contact."

The superintendent's application to the facilities commission pointed out that environmental studies "show extensive and severe surface and subsurface soil contamination in many areas utilized by the students, including the athletic fields, practice areas and the agricultural activities area."

The school district is currently gathering evidence for a possible lawsuit against the Army Corps of Engineers.

The governor was not at home during the candlelight vigil, but state troopers guarding the residence promised to deliver the newly drafted executive order to him. Many of the demonstrators vowed to stay all night in order to make their plea to the governor in person before the schools opened the next morning.

August 24, 2000

Secrets Of The Atomic Schools

There's an untold story behind the almost $24 million Marion's River Valley School District will receive in the next three years. The U.S. government, through an act of Congress, promised $15 million to build a new high school and middle school, while the state enacted legislation kicking in an additional $8.9 million to the district, which also plans to build two elementary schools.

The $15 million from the armed services budget is explained easily enough, as one concerned Marion resident told *Columbus Alive*: at least 12 River Valley alumni with leukemia multiplied by an average settlement of $1.25 million equals $15 million. The state's $8.9 million payment might be better explained as hush money for the questionable handling of the polluted site the River Valley Schools were built upon.

Despite the site's toxic legacy—which dates as far back as the dawn of the atomic age in the 1940s, when the land was an Army engineers' depot—public officials are hesitant to jump to any conclusions about the leukemia cases and unusual cancer rates suffered by River Valley alumni. The Ohio Department of Health is examining case studies to see if there is a link between the contamination and disease. In the meantime, middle and high school students literally sit in the middle of the uncertainty—their parents knowing all too well of studies which have indicated abnormally high cancer rates among graduates.

To put it mildly, the recent years have been tense ones for Governor Bob Taft, Ohio EPA officials and state and federal legislators, as they scrambled to find a solution to the problems in the small city just an hour's drive north of Columbus. When federal and state officials cut a deal earlier this year that allowed the U.S. and Ohio governments to kick in money for relocation of the schools—provided Marion residents kick in almost $20 million with a property tax levy of their own—they breathed a sigh of relief.

"For months the state has been working with the [Army] Corps [of Engineers] and Senators [George] Voinovich and [Mike] DeWine to craft a solution to the very complex situation in Marion," Taft said in a May 2000 Ohio Department of Health press release. "With this agreement, River Valley students and families will receive a new school facility and the community will have a significant tract of land available for industrial development."

But according to an extensive review of documents obtained by *Columbus Alive*, the schools' toxic problem isn't as new as the politicians would probably like to believe. The Ohio EPA knew of contamination on the site for more than two decades, and information on the site's role in the Manhattan Project was discovered by an environmental audit team in the late 1980s.

In three years the kids will be moved to new schools and the dump will be cleaned up by the U.S. Army Corps of Engineers so it can be re-used for industrial purposes. Cleaning its former depot site to industrial standards will cost the Army Corps $5 million to $10 million. To move the children temporarily, clean the dump to residential standards, and move the students back into the schools would have cost substantially more—$44.5 million.

Clearly the armed services are smiling at the price tag. They're the ones responsible for the mess in the first place.

Despite claims to the contrary, the Ohio Environmental Protection Agency knew at least 22 years ago that the River Valley Junior High and High School property was formerly an Army engineers' depot, with a contaminated dump directly next to the school property. Correspondence dating to 1978 between Plant City Steel, the Marion County Health Department and the Ohio EPA's district office in Bowling Green specifically addressed a toxic dump just south of the schools' fence line. At the time, Plant City Steel was dumping toxic waste on a site adjacent to the River Valley Schools property.

In 2000, Howard L. Jones, a 1978 River Valley graduate, wrote the Marion County Health Department requesting information related to the dumping of toxic waste near the River Valley Schools. Marion County Director of Environmental Health Lowell Lufkin responded in a May 1 letter: "Mr. Phil Case was the director of environmental health for the Marion County Health Department for many years. Shortly after Mr. Case left the department all the files for nuisance violations and solid waste violations were lost."

So Lufkin turned to the Ohio EPA's Northwest District Office for the requested information—material on toxic dumping at the school site that the Ohio EPA had long denied knowledge of—and the EPA office sent it.

Within the information Lufkin received and forwarded to Jones was a clear and disturbing photograph of an open waste dump dated July 26, 1978, with a handwritten note on the back: "Marion County Plant City Steel dump located on the old Marion Ordinance Depot."

Also included in the EPA material was a letter dated July 7, 1978, that Case sent William Walters, the Plant City Steel plant manager, demanding that the steel company "cease operation of your disposal site immediately." Case wrote, "You must either dig a trench and bury all waste or haul enough dirt in to cover the area with two feet of dirt cover."

Ten days later, the steel company's attorney, Walter D. Moore, wrote promising that Plant City Steel would "henceforth refrain" from using the dump near the schools, but the company refused to "bury or cover the waste present" at the site since "the land on which the dump is located is owned by some segment of the government." Moreover, Moore insisted, "The company was given permission to use the dump...[and] that Plant City was only one of a number of users of the dump."

That same month, Moore again wrote Case, informing him that the Ohio EPA had made "demands of Plant City that it cannot fulfill." Moore claimed that the dump site land was owned by the U.S. General Service Administration (GSA), and was "immediately supervised by 83rd [U.S. Army] ARCOM, Ft. Hayes, Columbus, Ohio."

Case informed the Ohio EPA that he had "contacted Mr. James F. Lyons, GSA, and explained the Plant City dump problems." Case's letter also notes that "He [Lyons] is contacting his legal adviser and is getting some up-to-date maps from Chicago, then he will come up and look over the problem."

Ohio EPA District Chief R.J. Manson wrote Walters on August 4 that year informing him that the agency's investigation had found two violations: "Operating a solid waste facility without plan approval and an operating license" and "Operating an open dump and open burning."

By November 22, 1978, the Ohio EPA had apparently solved the problem of the toxic waste site. "The road leading into this area has been barricaded. The Ohio National Guard plans to cover the area with dirt," revealed an internal EPA letter. The letter did not explain how the dirt would keep the toxins from migrating onto the adjacent school property.

Environmental concerns with the Marion schools site emerged again a decade later, with even more ominous implications. On March 21, 1988, Benatec Associates Inc. issued an environmental audit report commissioned by the HARSCO Corporation regarding the sale of the company's Plant City Steel (PCS) operation in Marion. The steel company had purchased the audited property in 1966 from the U.S. government, and ceased operations in 1986.

In order to determine how the government had used the site prior to 1966, Benatec researchers contacted, among others, James F. Lyons, then the facility's manager for the U.S. GSA in Columbus.

The Benatec report noted, "Mr. Lyons stated that to the best of his knowledge, part of the depot was used for storage, bomb production, and experiments regarding the development of the first atomic bomb."

Lyons suggested that Benatec researchers contact Charles Mosher, the author of a recent book titled *The Scioto Ordnance Plant and the Marion Engineer Depot of Marion, Ohio: A Profile After Forty Years*. Mosher claimed "that portions of 'The Manhattan Project' for the development of the first atomic bomb were conducted exclusively in a building on the depot and off the now PCS property."

"Mr. Mosher stated that he was personally involved in 'The Manhattan Project.' He suggested that Mr. Robert Ferguson of Marion, Ohio, former safety director of the Marion depot, be contacted," the Benatec report added.

In a telephone interview with a Benatec investigator, Ferguson verified that he worked in the depot's fire department between 1948 and 1954, and served as the facility's safety director between 1954 and 1960. "According to Mr. Ferguson, a concrete building west of the water tower and south of Route 309 contained radioactive material utilized for 'The Manhattan Project' during World War II. He felt that the building known as Building 517 may have been used for the storage of radioactive material. Building 517 is presently on the western end of the PCS property. He further stated that a storm sewer ran from Warehouse No. 4 south of Route 309 to Building 510 and then in open ditches towards the river."

When contacted by *Columbus Alive* this week, Ferguson said he had no knowledge of the Manhattan Project, and the 1988 report must have misquoted him. Ferguson did confirm to *Alive* that radioactive materials were stored at the depot.

A deed from World War II substantiates the government's lease of the drainage ditch in question. "Allegedly, cattle and sheep in the area drinking from the open ditches were impacted and lawsuits against the government with out-of-court settlements resulted," the Benatec report read.

Ferguson also claimed "that there was a dump for 'nonsalvageable excess waste' which, prior to his personally stopping it, contained used solvent, paint, waste oil, etc."

The Benatec environmental audit found "five major areas of concern": three underground storage tanks near Building 510; "43 55-gallon drums stored on wooden pallets...full or partially filled" with what "may be lead and chromate enamel"; the storm drainage systems on the eastern and western ends of the property; the radioactive material storage areas, particularly Buildings 517 and 510; and "a general dump for waste material for the National Guard and the PCS operation."

In August 1988, Benatec issued a second report noting that "although the PCS operation and environmental records were destroyed, indications are that spray painting and storage of electric transformers containing PCBs may have occurred on the site."

"Forty-three barrels containing an oily substance had visibly spilled on the ground," the second report stated. In sampling the property for toxic and radioactive contamination, the Benatec investigators found "some level of volatile gases." As a result, "all involved personnel went to level-C protection. This consists of oil resistant Tyvek suits, gloves, boots and respirators." The meter reading for volatile organic compounds for environment sampling hole "D-4" was six times the limit that triggered level-C protection.

The Benatec samples showed that "a great deal of oil remains in the soil due to a past oil spill on the property."

The Ohio EPA began another investigation of the depot site in July 1989, which resulted in the agency filing a 33-count civil action on February 28, 1994, against Plant City Steel parent HARSCO for violation of Ohio environmental laws. The counts included the illegal operation of a hazardous waste facility, unlawful burning of hazardous waste, failure to mark hazardous waste containers, failure to analyze hazardous waste and failure to keep written operating records, among other charges. The Ohio EPA asked for $10,000 a day in fines. Within a week, HARSCO had settled for $100,000 and an agreement to close the waste dump.

The initial closure plan submitted to the EPA by HARSCO subsidiary Getman Brothers Manufacturing Company included 11 of 12 hazardous waste storage units. Jeff Steers of the Ohio EPA's Northwest District Office signed off as the group leader on the closure plan, but the EPA refused to accept the closure plan for one unit, Area L. The closure plan submitted to the Ohio EPA during Governor George Voinovich's administration for Area L was not finally approved until five years later, during Governor Bob Taft's administration—two years into the current River Valley Schools controversy.

Beginning in 1996, the state fire marshal ordered the Ohio Army National Guard to take benzene samples from the ground water at the Marion Army Guard site located on the old depot property, abutting River Valley Junior High School. The River Valley Schools' contamination crisis began the next year, the same year that HARSCO paid the Ohio EPA more than half a million dollars in a settlement for violation of air pollution control laws at a Marysville manufacturing facility.

The U.S. Army Corps of Engineers commissioned an Environmental Baseline Survey in 1996 of the Marion Outdoor Training Area, on the same former depot site near the school. The corps' study found "no definite hazardous waste or material...at the time of the site visit." The corps did find three empty drums "in the vicinity of a potential wetland area."

The brief report concluded, "After reviewing historical use documents of the site it is not known exactly what types of materials, if any, were stored at this location. According to existing data, facility records and current conditions there is no documented or physical evidence indicating hazardous materials were ever used or stored at this site."

Of course the Army's investigators could have simply walked over to the Marion Historical Society and purchased a copy of Mosher's book to find out that material for the Manhattan Project was stored there, along with radioactive infrared sniper scopes and radium disks, through the 1950s. Nazi prisoners of war resided there as well.

While state and federal officials tend to ignore, dismiss or downplay the Benatec report and Army Corps of Engineers findings in their ongoing investigation of the high rates of leukemia and cancers at River Valley's High School and Junior High, information continues to filter out suggesting a cover-up of the depot's past contamination.

A confidential letter arrived at the headquarters of the Ohio EPA, dated April 24, 1993. The author, Mary Prior, had worked at the depot from 1945 until it closed in 1961. She had a simple question: "Was there ever any effort made to determine what was buried at the site of the old Marion Engineer Depot?"

"It was part of my duty to order not only office supplies, but also items needed in the shop area, such as paint, paint thinner, paint remover, carbon tetrachloride (now a known carcinogen) and trichloroethylene (also now a known carcinogen)," Prior confessed. "Back then stuff was just buried somewhere on the post...It was poured on the ground near the building. The area must have been saturated...I know absolutely that it was disposed of because the drums always went back empty. Hundreds of gallons of trichloroethylene were disposed of out there because I used to order a drum several times a year."

"Several years ago I saw a *60 Minutes* broadcast about a company...which had not properly disposed of some trichloroethylene and it resulted in a number of illnesses in the area... A businessman who used to work out there said I should let sleeping dogs lie," Prior's letter ended, "But there is already a school on that old depot property and the warehouses are being used."

The River Valley High School opened in 1962 and the adjacent Junior High in 1968. In 1997, a River Valley School nurse reported to the Ohio Department of Health that a disproportionate number of leukemia cases had struck students and graduates. Between 1966 and 1995, leukemia death rates rose by 122 percent in the city of Marion, and brain cancer death rates increased by 40 percent in the county.

Cases of esophageal cancer is 10 times the normal rate in Marion, according to a Ohio Department of Health survey. *USA Today* reported in 2000 that a government study found a 40-percent increase in esophageal cancer among workers involved in early nuclear weapons production.

When the Ohio EPA checked the River Valley High School grounds in September 1997, the agency discovered a dime-sized radium disk in front of the school. The radioactive disks, stored at the former depot, were used as reflectors to highlight bridges and roadways during World War II. Between 50,000 and 80,000 of these disks were stored at the depot at one time, according to Charles Mosher's book and U.S. military documents. The military claimed the disks were moved, but can't provide the paperwork showing when or where the disks went. A few Marion parents suspect the radium disks were dumped and buried on the old depot site.

In the last week of June 1998, Army contractor Montgomery Watson conducted tests at various locations at the River Valley School property. The on-site laboratory picked up such a significant level of the carcinogenic chemical vinyl chloride that the testers dismissed it as "an apparent false detection."

To eliminate these assumed "false" readings of a potent carcinogen, the Montgomery Watson testers adjusted the temperature and then detected carbon disulfide, a lesser toxin. However, in the investigative results from one of the two field samples of "water from hole," the vinyl chloride numbers tested in the range of 700,000 times the allowable risk standard.

The Ohio EPA now tests air inside the schools every three months. The U.S. Army Corps of Engineers tests air quality outside the site monthly. Those tests, along with the Ohio EPA's and Army's groundwater and soil tests, have shown toxin levels not to be dangerous to human health, according to the EPA.

The Ohio EPA also attempted a more thorough historical evaluation after data from the Ohio Department of Health set off the current crisis. In October 1997, the EPA submitted a "Historical Aerial Photograph Analysis" spanning 1939 to 1966. The first photo submitted—dated August 31, 1961, just prior to the depot's closing by the Army—shows a strangely plowed triangle of land precisely where the junior high school now sits. Concerned parents fear this unexplained disturbed land may be a waste dump. The revealing photo was not made public by the EPA until January 1999.

That same month, the U.S. Army Corps of Engineers handed out status memos to the recently established citizens' Restoration Advisory Board for the Depot (RAB) recommending that no further action was necessary on the old Army dump site.

RAB would later hire its own expert, Bruce Molholt, a Ph.D. in microbiology who recommended, with the "demonstrated high disease frequency," that the school be relocated and that a "prolonged excavation of the dump" was "required." Molholt pointed to the 1997 leukemia mortality study showing that deaths had increased by 122 percent in Marion in the past 30 years.

The Ohio EPA discredited Molholt's and co-researcher J.R. Kolmer's findings in a September 2000 press release. "The consultants' epidemiology data inappropriately associated past cancer incidences of River Valley grads with current environmental conditions at the site," it said. The Ohio EPA also accused the researchers of having a limited understanding of the trichloroethylene breakdown process.

But when questioned about the 1961 photo, the Ohio EPA's Jeff Steers told the *Columbus Dispatch*, "This is new information... In earlier photos taken in the 1950s, it [the area under the school] wasn't disturbed at all."

Steers told the *Marion Star* in 1999 that the Ohio EPA came across the photo while digging through its Marion depot archives. He said, "I can't tell you when we actually got it [the 1961 aerial photo]."

The actual date the EPA received the photo, according to EPA's own files, is October 27, 1997. Steers explained to *Columbus Alive* that Lawhon and Associates, the company with which the Ohio EPA contracted, had found the photo during a records search, but Steers did not see it until 1999.

In 1998, Paul Jayko, of the Ohio EPA's Division of Emergency and Remedial Response, prepared a two-page analysis of an electromagnetic survey and seized upon two "anomalies." What Jayko saw were "buried metallic objects and possible waste materials having high electrical conductivity such as sludge of some type. The size and shape of the anomaly strongly suggests disposal of a waste material."

Jayko suggested the EPA move its testing directly to the other side of the River Valley School's chain-link fence, since "due to the limited mapping imposed by property boundaries, it is impossible to determine whether the mapped anomaly is shown in its entirety or is only the tip of the iceberg."

Jayko's January 8, 1998, internal memo was addressed to Steers. Whoever received the memo wrote the word "No" in felt pen and Xed out Jayko's recommendation to test the Army property next to the middle school.

Steers told *Columbus Alive* he was "not aware" of the memo.

Jayko's concerns were obvious. With students at the middle school and high school, he "suspected that any contaminant existing in this area has a direct pathway to the surface [due to the disruption of the clay soil by landfill activity] and there may be a dermal, ingestion and inhalation pathway." Jayko's map showed what he thought was an obvious toxic waste site approximately 300-feet-by-200-feet in size just in back of the school's fence.

During the summer of 1998, Jayko lost his position as Marion Site Director because of alleged poor performance. Recently, Judge Thomas F. Phalen Jr. ruled that the Ohio EPA "wanted to do something graduated and far less effective" than a full investigation at the Marion site. Phalen ruled that the Ohio EPA had broken federal whistle blower laws by disciplining and reassigning Jayko.

A little over a month after the Paul Jayko memo to Jeff Steers, Steers wrote a curious memo to Ohio EPA Director Donald Schregardus regarding the "Marion investigation." Steers indicated that the decision to do ambient air monitoring at the site would be left up to the U.S. Army Corps of Engineers, under the Department of Defense (DOD), which was responsible for the original pollution. Another goal would be to work with the Department of Energy (DOE), which was responsible for the radioactive contamination on the site. Steers added, "No Superfund money will be used since DOE and DOD are clearly the responsible parties and must pay for all associated costs of cleanup."

Montgomery Watson prepared a draft report for the Army Corps of Engineers in November 1998. In the brief four-page report, the contractor wrote: "The principal contaminant found was vinyl chloride, which is a breakdown product of trichloroethylene."

In February 1999, after concerned Marion residents charged

the depot contamination was being covered up, a much larger Army Corps of Engineers report with the same November 1998 date mysteriously appeared in the public repository of the Marion Public Library. The Corps was clearly retreating from its earlier "three empty barrels" analysis.

Montgomery Watson's assessment in the expanded report was straightforward. The "Overall Relative Risk: High" and the status of the Army's dump in back of the school property posed "imminent threats." Soldiers would no longer train in the area, and the report noted "ecological receptors [living organisms like mammals] have not been evidenced at this phase, however, there's a nature preserve on this parcel of land alleged to have been a waste disposal area."

The report fails to mention the ecological receptors—that is, students—standing directly on the other side of the chain-link fence.

Steers told the *Columbus Dispatch* that the Montgomery Watson report "was an internal document to justify funding requests. It was not to be circulated publicly."

The *Toledo Blade* reported in October 2000 that "Two-thirds of that 1953 dump [shown in the aerial photo] is River Valley School property. The other third is on the Army reserve training site which has been closed since 1999 because of health risks."

River Valley School Superintendent Thomas G. Shade rode to the Ohio EPA's rescue with a 1999 "The Voice of the Valley Environmental Bulletin." Shade told Marion parents that newly discovered toxic waste barrels were 500 to 800 yards beyond the fence that separates the school from the reserve ground. A *Columbus Alive* analysis of Army Corps of Engineers maps and other public documents indicates that the superintendent mistook yards for feet in his apparent effort to calm parents. In fact, the dump was as close as 500 feet to school property.

When later asked about the mix-up, Shade told *Alive*, "I can't tell you if it was yards or feet."

Shade also told parents, "The school and local government officials found out about the barrels on the reserve grounds when the public did—two months after the U.S. Army Reserve learned about them."

Apparently the Ohio EPA or the federal government failed to tell Shade about the Benatec study or Prior's 1993 letter or even the 1978 dump investigation. Indeed, Shade told *Alive* that he hadn't read the Benatec report and that Prior's name simply "rings a bell."

Governor Bob Taft's new EPA director, Chris Jones, tried a different approach. In a memo to the governor, he wrote, "The contaminated area has been there for years, and the public knew it existed." Thankfully Jones knew the difference between yards and feet, noting that the area was "500-800 feet from the school fence line."

While Shade was publicly calming parents, albeit with shaky information, he was also submitting an application from the River Valley Local School District to Ohio's Extreme Environmental Contamination Program for funds to build new schools. In the 1999 application he wrote, "Surface soil contamination contains unacceptable levels of carcinogenic polyaromatic hydrocarbons including benzo a pyrene. The paths of exposure include inhalation, ingestion and dermal contact."

Publicly, the superintendent followed the government's line, telling the *Marion Star* in February 1999 "that the trenching in front of the middle school did not indicate the school was built on top of a dump site."

Shade's efforts did not go unnoticed. In a February 2000

"Privileged/Confidential" memo obtained by *Alive*, EPA Director Jones wrote to Superintendent Shade, "I appreciate the effort you are making to 'keep the noise down.' I really believe that it will be to everyone's benefit in the long run."

Shade had written Jones a February 9, 2000, "heads up" on a possible story by *Columbus Dispatch* reporter Jill Ripenhoff. Shade told Jones: "Again, to the degree possible we are trying to be sensitive to the whole issue, keep the noise down and proceed accordingly."

Shade told *Columbus Alive* that these memos shouldn't be taken out of context. A time of sensitive negotiations is not the time to start venting in local newspapers, he said.

"You don't go into negotiations that had just started with the Army Corps of Engineers and the Ohio EPA," Shade said. "You don't go into negotiations in good faith and out the back door go out blasting people."

The superintendent added, "Those memos were in that vein...not trying to cover up anything or hide anything."

While politicians and school leaders are busy defending their actions, grassroots groups like Ohio Citizen Action and Concerned River Valley Families continue to pressure Governor Bob Taft to remove children to another location. Citizens and activists have presented the governor with thousands of letters and documentation of the problems in Marion. "His complete inaction speaks for itself," Citizen Action's Simona Vaclavikova said of the governor. The group is not satisfied with the promise of a better tomorrow—when new schools are built in three years—while kids sit in the schools today.

Taft spokesperson Troy Kirkpatrick said of those letters, only 14 actually came from residents of the River Valley. Many letters didn't supply a return address.

Just prior to the November election, Stephen Lester, the science director at the Center for Health, Environment and Justice, analyzed the data from the River Valley School property and concluded with a simple question: "I have to raise a common sense question that I cannot answer. Why are the students still attending this school? The RI [U.S. Army's Remedial Investigation] report, even with its limitations, still shows serious hot spots on the school site." The River Valley School officials had earlier taken action by not allowing students to use the back exits of the school.

Vaclavikova said the fact that the bond issue to raise money for new schools passed this November is evidence Marion residents fear for the safety of their children.

"Obviously there's chemicals on the property and that's well-publicized," the Ohio EPA's Jeff Steers said. But, he points out that all EPA tests have indicated that the levels are not dangerous to human health.

River Valley Superintendent Shade told *Alive* that until case studies are completed by the Ohio Department of Health, no one should jump to conclusions. "The concern is, is it safe now?" Shade asked. He said it's "irresponsible" to make linkages between the rate of leukemia among people who went to the schools 10 years ago and possible dangers today. "We've relied on safety and the scientific method from the inception of this problem." Shade pointed out that all but one of River Valley's school board members has children or grandchildren at the junior high school or high school—not to mention the fact that Shade roams the halls regularly.

"What ulterior motive could there be for me to work on a campus that I thought was unsafe?" Shade asked. "We absolutely, firmly, confidently maintain that this campus is safe."

Taft and others maintain that the unusual Marion bond issue with matching state and federal money was an all-encompassing package intended to deal with ailing elementary schools as well as environmental problems at the high school and junior high school. Taft spokesperson Kirkpatrick mentioned Taft's visit to Caledonia Elementary School: "Their computer center where they kept all their servers was in the bathroom."

But at the junior high and high schools, an unseen, more unsightly problem lurks deep underneath the soil.

With their funding locked up, officially all is well in Marion, despite the fact that River Valley Junior High School children will go to school on a toxic waste site for the next three years, while a new school is being built, and their nearby high school neighbors will continue to play on contaminated ground.

Co-written with Jamie Pietras
December 7, 2000

Reading, 'Riting And Radioactivity

One way to look at the atomic secrets buried under Marion's River Valley Schools is that the kids and educators were simply collateral damage of the Cold War. For years, bits and pieces of Ohio's major role in the Manhattan Project and the thermonuclear arms race have been dribbling out in the media. Here's a quick refresher course.

The uranium processing plant in Fernald—18 miles northwest of Cincinnati—was so contaminated by radiation that state and federal agencies barred their inspectors from visiting the plant in 1989. The Fernald plant was opened in 1952 by the U.S. Atomic Energy Commission to produce nuclear bomb-grade uranium.

The *St. Louis Post-Dispatch* wrote in 1989, "Ohio officials say that in the 37 years it has been in operation, the plant has released 298,000 pounds of uranium waste into the air and 167,000 pounds of waste into the Greater Miami River. Another 12.7 million pounds of waste were put into pits, which may be leaking. And the plant's concrete storage tanks are cracked and leaking. Leaking radioactivity has contaminated the Greater Miami Aquifer, which supplies drinking water to about two million people in the Cincinnati area. The plant sits on the aquifer."

Of course, things could have been worse. In 1993, at the unrelated Fernald State School in Waltham, Massachusetts, the *Boston Globe* reported that scientists from Harvard University and MIT fed radioactive forms of iron and calcium to 19 mentally retarded boys in their breakfast milk to monitor the health effects. Their parents were told they were in a "science club."

In the January 1994 *Columbus Free Press* story "Battelle and the Banality of Evil," the muckraking paper pointed out that the institute had played a key role in the U.S. atomic and nuclear programs and that the Department of Defense estimated it would take more than $100 million in radioactive cleanup costs alone at Battelle's facilities.

The next month, the *Free Press* interviewed a moon-suited environmental decontamination worker leaving Battelle's West Jefferson site and published that there was radioactive contamination from an experimental laboratory and reactor. Battelle refused to comment but soon categorically denied the charge to the now-defunct *Columbus Guardian*.

The *Columbus Dispatch*'s Scott Powers, perhaps the state's best environmental reporter, managed to confirm the radioactive contamination in a June 1994 story bizarrely headlined "Battelle to clean up soil; Lab dust may be responsible for contamination." Battelle's Vice President, Kenneth Brog, reassured central Ohio residents by noting, "We certainly don't want to give anyone the impression that this plutonium, which is trapped in soils, migrates readily."

Essential reading is Powers' October 1995 *Dispatch* article reporting that Ohio has "around 50 documented radioactive sites," more than any other state. Along with Fernald, the Mound Laboratory in Miamisburg and the Portsmouth Gaseous Diffusion Plant near Piketon were part of the "Big

Three" nasties. The estimated cost of cleaning up these sites is well over $20 billion.

Earlier this year, *Dispatch* reporter Randall Edwards wrote, "For nearly 40 years, Battelle scientists using the same mechanical arms unlocked the secrets of atomic energy, first for use in powerful bombs, then for more peaceful causes." The article also pointed out that "Fuel rods and equipment from these plants [nuclear power plants] were shipped to West Jefferson for three decades, and as a result, many of the buildings there became contaminated with radioactivity."

It's not uncommon to find Manhattan Project contamination in urban areas, even outside research facilities like Battelle. The *Dispatch*'s Powers revealed, "For eight months in 1943, B&T Metals at 425 W. Town St. was one of numerous small machine shops secretly pressed into service to manufacture uranium pellets for the Manhattan Project." In 1996, the U.S. government undertook an estimated $2.3 million clean-up of radioactive dust at the plant site.

The discovery of radioactive contamination directly linked to the Manhattan Project at two Dayton Board of Education buildings, including the Green Jr. ROTC Academy, stirred controversy in Dayton in 1998.

During the Fernald cleanup, medical experts suggested that the radium, linked specifically to leukemia, be cleaned up first as a health threat. Ohio Environmental Protection Agency officials found a dime-sized radium-coated disk in front of Marion's River Valley Schools in September 1997.

Soon after, the *Dispatch*'s Frank Hinchey raised the radium and radiation issue at the schools, pointing to the radioactive contamination in Building 517 at the Marion Engineering Depot and the "about 58,000 radium markers stored at the depot." Reportedly, the radium disks were shipped to the

Aberdeen Proving Grounds in Maryland after World War II, claimed the Army Corps of Engineers.

One of the reasons that military-related toxic and radioactive waste keeps showing up at schools results from the Federal Property and Administrative Service Act of 1949, enacted to sell off surplus government property, particularly for public use such as schools. A decade ago, parents of high school students in St. Charles County, Missouri, were shocked when the government attempted to open up an old uranium and thorium plant half a mile from the Francis Howell High School. Wherever you find a school on an old military base or installation, public officials would be wise to check for toxic or radioactive contamination.

December 14, 2000

An Open Letter
To The United Nations

Recently, President George W. Bush addressed your august assembly. Despite obtaining his office by what appeared to be a fraudulent coup—and stealing the electoral votes of the state of Florida, where his brother Jeb is governor—he did make one impressive point: "Our principles and our security are challenged today by outlaw groups and regimes that accept no law of morality and have no limit to their violent ambitions."

The U.N. needs to realize that Bush's statement is a Freudian slip—a self-confession about the real terrorist network that surrounds him in Washington, D.C.

In December 1983, once and future Defense Secretary Donald Rumsfeld traveled to Iraq to extend his hand of friendship to Saddam Hussein. Rumsfeld, then a private citizen, was acting as a liaison for the Reagan-Bush administration.

As we say in U.S. politics, they knew Saddam was a son-of-a-bitch, but they wanted him "as our son-of-a-bitch."

You know the history here—Somoza, Pappa Doc Duvalier, the Shah of Iran, Marcos, Franco. These are just a few of a long list of fascists and thugs employed by the U.S. to do its imperialist bidding. Saddam was viewed as just another pawn to settle scores with the Iranian people, who had rightfully overthrown their brutal dictator, the Shah.

In November 2002, Senator Robert Byrd released documents showing that the U.S. sent biological weapons to their then-friend Saddam throughout the 1980s. This includes anthrax and West Nile virus, among other nasty pathogens.

Also, the U.S.'s trusted British allies sent Saddam anthrax through its lab Porten Down. Never to be left far behind, it's well-documented from the Gulf War that the Germans chipped in by helping build facilities that could produce chemical weapons for Iraq. Much of this was recently reported in that radical publication *Newsweek*.

Moreover, President Bush had well-established ties to the former al Qaeda bank of choice, the now-defunct BCCI, the Bank of Credit and Commerce International. You might want to consult the *Wall Street Journal*, which revealed the connections between the BCCI drugs, arms and terrorist network and Bush's Harken Oil.

Bush's current obsession with Saddam Hussein may be to throw us off the trail of his and his father's old buddy Osama bin Laden. As the BBC reported earlier this year, a secret FBI document, numbered 1991 WF213589, from its Washington field office, shows how President Bush removed FBI agents from the bin Laden family trail while the al Qaeda terrorist network planned their attacks on the World Trade Center.

The U.N. needs to look at the strange relationship between Saudi Arabia, Pakistan and the United States. Instead of focusing on whether or not someone from Iraq met once with someone in al Qaeda, why not look at the obvious? Fifteen of the 19 hijackers were Saudis. One of the masterminds behind the attack, Mohammed Atta, was working for the CIA's ally, the Pakistan Intelligence Service (ISI). More obviously, this terrorist network and the whole "jihaddi" ideology was manufactured by U.S. intelligence, paid for by the Saudis, and the recruits trained in Pakistan's Madressas.

While you're at it, the Security Council might want to delve into the small private company where George Bush the Elder now works, the Carlyle Corporation, which appears to be reaping huge profits from the U.S. military buildup. Instead of worrying about whether Saddam is trying to develop a bomb, the Security Council should focus on Pakistan, which has developed a nuclear device and recently threatened to use it against India.

As Pulitzer Prize-winning writer Seymour Hersh detailed earlier this year in the *New Yorker*, the United States Special Forces in Afghanistan evacuated al Qaeda and Pakistani ISI forces to Kashmir. Terrorist activity soon followed, bringing the world to the brink of nuclear exchange between Pakistan and India.

I would also like to reiterate that the Bush administration is proud of its imperialist plans to dominate the globe, and even publishes its intentions online. You might want to start with the military plan "Joint Vision for 2020," which calls for "full spectrum dominance" using space weapons. Also, I recommend an Air Force research paper "Weather as a force multiplier: Owning the weather in 2025."

And, before I forget, an April 1996 Air Force research paper "Alternative futures for 2025: Security planning to avoid surprise" points out in a scenario called "Gulliver's Travails" how a terrorist attack in the early 21st century would make it possible to galvanize the U.S. people into getting behind Bush's dream of a new Roman Empire.

Oh, and one more thing: You already know how important that terrorist attack was to the madmen in Washington. Zbigniew Brzezinski outlined the significance of such an event in his 1997 book *The Grand Chessboard*. Unless the U.N. acts now to stop Bush's smiley-faced fascism, we'll have another Hitler on our hands.

Columbus Free Press
November 13, 2002

1441 And Fight

As if to celebrate the new year, the Bush administration entered 2003 by ordering a predictable post-Christmas call-up of U.S. troops. President George W. Bush is busy resurrecting the discredited doctrine of "preventative" war to justify an attack on Iraq. "Preventative" war was last invoked by Nazi Party leaders as a defense of their actions during the Nuremberg trials.

The U.S. government is engaging in an unprecedented propaganda campaign to justify its invasion and occupation of Iraq. Our government's plans to seize 119 billion barrels of known Iraqi oil reserves are conveniently ignored.

Still, the reality of selling the Iraq war is proving difficult, especially since Iraq has no nuclear weapons, and its only known link to biochemical weapons were those supplied by the U.S. and its allies during the 1980s.

While the U.S. points fingers at Iraq, the press routinely reports that the Bush's chief Islamic ally in the region, Pakistan, provided the nuclear technology to North Korea. So, Pakistan, a major nuclear power, with direct ties to al Qaeda and the North Korean nuclear weapons program, is not a threat, according to Bush.

At Bush's insistence, the United Nations Security Council passed Resolution 1441 on November 8, 2002. A preambulatory clause in Resolution 1441 references "the threat Iraq's noncompliance with Council resolutions and proliferation of weapons of mass destruction and long-range missiles poses to international peace and security."

A key operative clause in the resolution required Iraq, "not later than 30 days from the date of this resolution, [to submit] a current, accurate, full and complete declaration of all aspects of its programs to develop chemical, biological and nuclear weapons." The resolution endorses unrestricted access by U.N. weapons inspectors to any Iraqi sites and "warns Iraq that it will face serious consequences...for failure to comply."

The resolution stands in sharp contrast to a lack of similar actions that could have been taken against the U.S., Pakistan or Israel, all with well-documented weapons of mass destruction programs.

Iraq had until November 15 to pledge compliance. Iraq complied with the inspections and, by December 8, Iraq, as required, provided the U.N. weapons inspectors and the Security Council "with a complete declaration of all aspects of its chemical, biological and nuclear programs."

Phyllis Bennis, fellow at the Institute for Policy Studies, argues, "This sets Iraq up with a 'damned if you do, damned if you don't' situation. If they claim they have no WMD [weapons of mass destruction] material to declare, Washington will find that evidence of the continuing 'breach' based on the U.S. assertion that Iraq does have viable WMD programs. If Iraq actually declares viable WMD programs, it similarly proves the U.S. claim of continuing breach of Resolution 687."

Richard Perle, chair of the U.S. Defense Policy Board, underscored Bennis' assertion when he confessed to the British Parliament that the U.S.'s plan to attack Iraq even if U.N. weapons inspectors gave the country a "clean bill of health," reported Britian's *Mirror* on November 24. Perle's admission caused Member of Parliament Peter Kilfoyle, a former Defense Minister, to remark, "America is duping the world into believing it supports these inspections. President Bush intends to go to war even if inspections find nothing."

White House Chief of Staff Andrew Card told NBC's *Meet The Press*: "We have the authority by the President's desire to protect and defend the United States of America. The U.N. can meet and discuss but we don't need their permission."

With the U.S. and UK enforcing a no-fly zone over approximately two-thirds of Iraqi territory, the case for strong action against Iraq remains puzzling.

President Bush outlined his case against Saddam Hussein and Iraq to the American people in a televised speech on October 7, 2002. Bush warned of the "clear evidence of peril" if Iraq decided to give chemical and biological weapons to terrorists. Bush did not discuss the perils involved with the U.S.'s prior policy of giving biological and chemical weapons to Saddam in the 1980s.

On the same day Bush was presenting his charges against Iraq to the American people, CIA Director George Tenet wrote a letter to Congress explaining that "Baghdad for now appears to be drawing a line short of conducting terrorist attacks with conventional or CBW [chemical or biological warfare] against the U.S., should Saddam conclude that a U.S.-led attack could no longer be deterred, he probably would become much less constrained in adopting terrorist actions."

The CIA's former head of counterintelligence told the London *Guardian*, "Basically, cooked information is working its way into high-level pronouncements and there's a lot of unhappiness about it in intelligence, especially among analysts at the CIA."

CIA Director Tenet's assessment stands in direct contrast to President Bush's assertion in his October 7 speech that "Iraq could decide on any given day to provide a biological or chemical weapon to a terrorist group or individual terrorists."

Britain's *Sunday Herald* detailed "Why the CIA Thinks Bush is Wrong," noting that Tenet's October 7 letter specifically spelled out that Bush's invasion policy might have adverse consequences: "Saddam might decide that the extreme step of assisting Islamic terrorists in conducting a WMD attack against the U.S. would be his last chance to exact vengeance by taking a large number of victims with him."

Thus, the new Bush doctrine establishes that any country possessing weapons of mass destruction or, alternatively, chemical and biological weapons, and possibly motivated to attack another nation at some unforeseen time in the future, should be subjected to preventative strikes by the U.S. unilaterally or after failure to comply with a U.N. Security Council resolution demanding immediate inspections.

Between the September 11, 2001, attacks on the World Trade Center and Pentagon, and Bush's October 7, 2002, speech, the U.S. had attempted to establish a *casus belli* for attacking Iraq despite the Bush's administration assertion that the September 11th attacks were perpetrated by Saddam's sworn enemy and arch-rival, Osama bin Laden and his al Qaeda network.

Reporter Gary Leupp noted, "First they [the U.S.] seized upon the story, which initially surfaced in a *Newsweek* report on September 19 [2001], that there had been a meeting between hijacker Mohammed Atta and Iraqi intelligence officers, including Farouk Hijaze, Iraq's ambassador to Turkey in Prague in June of 2000."

Leupp points out that had not "both British and Czech intelligence services" publicly "refuted" the story, the U.S. may have had justification for retaliating against Iraq. Moreover, Leupp suggests that the early U.S. attempts to link the anthrax attack to Iraqi laboratories, later discounted, was the U.S. in search of a cause, any cause, for war.

Francis A. Boyle, a University of Illinois professor of law, points out, "There is no evidence that Iraq was involved in the events on September 11... They are fishing around for some other justification to go to war with Iraq. They have come up with the doctrine of preemptive attack." Boyle notes that the doctrine of preemptive attack "was rejected by the Nuremberg tribunal" after lawyers for Nazi defendants used it to defend the actions of Germany's Third Reich.

James Rubin, the Assistant Secretary of State during the Clinton administration, analyzed the dangers of President Bush's new national security strategy in October 2002. He wrote: "The problem with the Bush document is that it appears to make first strikes the rule rather than the exception."

While the Bush administration stressed its multilateralism by pointing to the U.N. Security Council's adoption of Resolution 1441, the *New York Times* reported that prior to the adoption of the resolution, U.S. pilots were already bombing southern Iraq on practice runs. The *Times* reported, "Now, the Navy pilots gain combat experience when they police the no-flight zone. They have the chance to practice bombing tactics when the Iraqis refrain from firing at the patrols and to hone their skills in case of war."

With such U.S. tactics, it's not surprising that the *Washington Post* reported that "Fear of U.S. Power Shapes Iraq Debate."

In August 2002, a Knight Ridder article disclosed that Defense Secretary Donald Rumsfeld's staff had created a special planning unit for the invasion of Iraq. The story detailed how Deputy Secretary of Defense Paul Wolfowitz was working with a group primarily composed of civilians to launch an invasion of Iraq.

"The Bush administration began its campaign for a new resolution at about the same time it unveiled its national security doctrine, which outlines the concept of preemptive action to counter perceived threats," according to the *Post*. "The new doctrine unnerved even close allies who feared that the world's only superpower no longer felt bound by the international rules established after World War II."

By applying the Bush administration's new doctrine of preemptive military strikes, a strong case can be made that the U.N. Security Council needs to take action against the U.S.

First, there's ample evidence that the U.S. government or its intelligence apparatus created and protected Osama bin Laden prior to the 9/11 attacks. Professor Michael Chossudovsky, a bin Laden biographer and director of the Centre for Research on Globalization, holds that, "Lost in the barrage of recent history, the role of the CIA in supporting and developing international terrorist organizations during the Cold War and its aftermath is casually ignored or downplayed by the Western media."

Richard Labeviere echoes these sentiments in his book *Dollars for Terror: The U.S. and Islam*. Relying heavily on European intelligence sources, Labeviere argues that bin Laden and the al Qaeda network was "nurtured and encouraged by the U.S. intelligence community, especially during the Clinton years." He further asserts that bin Laden "was protected because the network was designed to serve U.S. foreign policy and military interests."

By taking a broader geostrategic approach, Labeviere contends, "The policy of guiding the evolution of Islam and of helping them against our adversaries worked marvelously well in Afghanistan against the Red Army. The same doctrines can still be used to destabilize what remains of Russian power, and especially to counter the Chinese influence in Central Asia."

If the U.N. Security Council would focus on U.S. relationships to bin Laden rather than more dubious links between Iraq's Saddam Hussein and his arch-rival, a case could be made for U.N. Security Council action against the U.S. The authoritative *Jane's Intelligence Digest* reported that, "Back in March [2001], Moscow's Permanent Mission at the U.N. submitted to the U.N. Security Council an unprecedentedly detailed report on al Qaeda's terrorist infrastructure in Afghanistan, but the U.S. government opted not to act."

The French daily *Le Figaro*—ironically owned by U.S. defense contractor the Carlyle Group, which employs former president George H.W. Bush—reported in October 2001 that bin Laden received treatment at the American hospital in Dubai, one of the United Arab Emirates, in July 2001. Moreover, *Le Figaro* reported that bin Laden met with a top CIA official while being treated at the American hospital.

The *Le Figaro* article raises the question of how bin Laden, eligible for execution for his alleged attacks on the *U.S.S. Cole* and the deaths of U.S. sailors, could reportedly fly out of Dubai on a private jet with no Navy fighters waiting to force him down and take him into custody.

The *Toronto Star* suggested, "One possible conclusion is that the bin Laden terror problem was allowed to get out of hand because bin Laden himself had powerful protectors in both Washington and Saudi Arabia."

There's enough evidence for the Security Council to investigate U.S. ties to bin Laden and al Qaeda as well as to look into whether the U.S. Department of Defense was planning a pre-emptive strike against Iraq before any legal basis was estab-lished under international law. By Bush administration stan-dards, the U.S. may have created a precedent that could be later used against itself for its long-standing relationships with bin Laden that reportedly continued until less than two months before the 9/11 terrorist attacks.

Since the Bush administration's efforts have proved success-ful in pressuring the U.N. Security Council to adopt Resolution 1441 regarding weapons inspections in Iraq, concerning Iraq's possible possession of chemical and biological weapons or other weapons of mass destruction, the body might want to broaden the inspectors' to-do list to include other countries with related programs. To get started, they wouldn't need to travel far beyond the U.N.'s New York headquarters.

In September 2002, U.S. Senator Robert C. Byrd, a Democrat from West Virginia, went public with documents obtained from the federal government establishing the U.S.'s role in the development of Iraq's biochemical program in the 1980s. Byrd told the *Charleston Gazette*, "We have in our hands the equivalent of a Betty Crocker cookbook of ingredients that the U.S. allowed Iraq to obtain and that may well have been used to concoct biological weapons."

Between 1985 and 1988, the nonprofit American Type Culture Collection, following the approval of the U.S. govern-ment, sent 11 shipments to Iraq that included anthrax, botu-linum toxin and gangrene. Also, between January 1980 and October 1993, the U.S. Centers for Disease Control shipped a variety of biological and toxic specimens to Iraq including West Nile virus and Dengue fever, according to the *Gazette*.

Senator Byrd's release of the information followed state-ments from Secretary of Defense Donald Rumsfeld that he had no knowledge of any such shipments in testimony before the Arms Services Committee.

In 1984, a United Nations report alleged that chemical weapons had been used by Iraq against Iran. The *New York Times* reported from Baghdad that, then-former Secretary of State Donald Rumsfeld was in Iraq as an envoy for President George H.W. Bush. The *Times* wrote, "American diplomats pronounced themselves satisfied with relations between Iraq and the U.S. and suggest that normal diplomatic ties have been restored in all but name."

U.S. Representative Dennis Kucinich wrote that "During the administration of Ronald Reagan, 60 helicopters were sold to Iraq. Later reports said Iraq used U.S.-made helicopters to spray Kurds with chemical weapons. According to the *Washington Post*, Iraq used mustard gas against Iran with the help of intelligence from the CIA."

In a forthcoming paper in the scientific journal *Bulletin of Atomic Scientists*, Professor of International Security Malcolm Dando and Mark Wheelis, a microbiologist, put forth the thesis that U.S. actions are undermining the 1972 biological weapons conventions in order to continue secret U.S. research on biological weapons. "They also point to the paradox of the U.S. developing such weapons at a time when it is proposing military action against Iraq on the grounds that Iraq is breaking international treaties," wrote the *Guardian* in a preview of the forthcoming article.

Thus, there's more than enough evidence to warrant an inspection of U.S. sites possibly involved with the Iraqi biological and chemical weapons program.

The U.S. poses a much greater threat to the world than Iraq through its weapons of mass destruction programs and delivery systems. If the U.N. Security Council compares Iraq, currently with no nuclear arsenal, to the U.S., with an extensive military nuclear arsenal and the only country to have used atomic weapons against civilians, then Resolution 1441 applies more to the U.S. than Iraq.

Columbus Free Press
January 2003

NAZIS

Whiny Dems And Jews

From Cincinnati's Riverfront Stadium to Columbus' Riffe Center, anti-Semitism is in vogue. But in the state capital, instead of chastising the bigot, we literally fire the messenger. Ask Devon Rice.

On May 8, 1996, at approximately 8:30 a.m., Rice, a messenger with the Legislative Service Commission, was delivering forms to House Speaker Jo Ann Davidson's office on the 14th floor when he heard Ohio House Sergeant-at-Arms Robert Foster loudly proclaim: "The Jews are just like the Democrats, all they do is whine."

After Foster "repeated himself several times," Rice confronted the Statehouse official and said, "Could you do me a favor, next time you make anti-Semitic remarks, could you lower your voice so I don't have to hear you?"

Rice says Foster initially denied that his remarks were anti-Semitic and reluctantly offered a half-hearted apology. Rice then dashed off a letter to Speaker Davidson, a Republican from Reynoldsburg, informing her of the incident and stating: "As a citizen of Ohio, as a human being and as a 'Jew,' I felt compelled to inform the gentleman that I heard him, that I was offended, and that his behavior was intolerable." Foster was sitting at his desk in the reception area at the time the remarks were made.

Rice wrote, "I personally do not care what the Sergeant-at-

Arms says at home, at a bar, or on the golf course. However, this type of behavior clearly has no place within his official capacity as an employee of the Ohio House of Representatives. His behavior was, aside from being ignorant and offensive, unprofessional."

Speaker Davidson seemed to concur. She ordered an immediate inquiry into the matter. Foster admitted that he had called two specific groups—the ACLU and the Jewish Defense League—"whiners just like the Democrats." Foster denied he ever referred to "Jews" specifically. Nevertheless, Davidson concluded in a letter dated May 15, 1996, that Foster's conduct was "entirely inappropriate and should not be condoned in the House of Representatives." Davidson directed Carol S. Norris, the executive secretary of the Ohio House, "to verbally reprimand Mr. Foster for his 'inappropriate' comments."

A copy of her letter to Rice was forwarded to the director of the Legislative Service Commission, Robert Shapiro. Within a week, Rice was given his six-month evaluation and told that his services would no longer be needed after the session ended.

Instead of talking to Rice face-to-face, the evaluation from his immediate supervisor Eric Rodriguez and Office Manager Cathy Kamer was simply left on his desk. Rice claims every time he was five minutes late was suddenly highlighted, although no one had ever spoke to him about tardiness before. And, curiously, a vague reference to having "gone above a supervisor on one occasion" appeared.

Rice resigned after the evaluation, rather than finish the session, and he requested an exit interview with Kamer and Shapiro. When he showed up at the appointed time, he found State Trooper Sergeant Moore waiting to escort him out of the building. "It's insane. The trooper threatened me with arrest," Rice said.

Shapiro acknowledges that he saw Davidson's letter, but refused to give Kamer's or Rodriguez's names when asked who evaluated Rice or whether they had seen Davidson's letter. "I'm not going to help you, you'll have to find out yourself," Shapiro told me. Shapiro has been under fire for withholding corporate donation information from the press and the Legislative Service Commission.

Shapiro claims he was unaware of the state trooper incident and suggests "not so convincingly" that Rice's evaluation had nothing to do with the letter. A true professional.

May 28, 1996

Speaker Pro Temper

State Representative William G. Batchelder, a Republican from Medina, the Speaker Pro Tempore of the Ohio House, is a member of the little-known and highly secretive far-right Council for National Policy (CNP), according to author and investigative reporter Russ Bellant. Bellant says that "The CNP is attempting to create a concentration of power to rival and eventually eclipse traditional centers of power in the U.S."

Newsweek reported that the CNP's first executive director, Louisiana State Representative Woody Jenkins, told Council members, "I predict that one day before the end of this century, the Council will be so influential that no president, regardless of party or philosophy, will be able to ignore us or our concerns or shut us out of the highest levels of government."

Batchelder, who narrowly lost a bid to be Speaker of the Ohio House, bears close scrutiny in Bellant's opinion.

Chip Berlet, of Political Research Associates, agrees. Berlet points out that the CNP includes "a former Ku Klux Klan leader and others who champion segregationist policies." Berlet concedes that these charges may seem "shocking," yet can be easily verified. He describes the beliefs of the CNP members as "not only traditionally conservative, but also [ascribes to them] nativism, xenophobia, theories of racial superiority, sexism, homophobia, authoritarianism, militarism, reaction and in some cases, outright neo-fascism."

A quick check of Batchelder's political activities in the last year or so showed that he praised Cleveland Mayor Michael White as "a very courageous guy" after White attacked public employees' unions. He also sponsored legislation that the Audubon Society deemed anti-environmental. And, Batchelder re-wrote Ohio banking laws so that they were pro-banking and not in the best interest of Ohio consumers, according to consumer advocates.

Harvey Wasserman, senior nuclear adviser for Greenpeace, recalled that, after a pro-environmental commentary he did on WCBE, Batchelder wrote and accused him of being "in the fever swamps of the far left."

"What I remember about the tone of the letter," Wasserman added, "was all the nasty name-calling."

Bellant, author of *The Religious Right in Michigan Politics, The Coors Connection* and *Old Nazis, The New Right, and the Republican Party*, monitors ultra-right political organizations. Bellant says the "membership of the Council comprises the elite of the radical right in America" and that "many Council members would prefer that their participation not be made public."

During the Iran-Contra scandal, the *State Times* of Baton Rouge reported that Oliver North was a CNP member and quoted the CNP's Norman Blackwell, "The policy [of CNP] is that we don't discuss who attends the meetings or what is said. The Council for National Policy is a tax-exempt 501(c)3 membership organization."

Bellant says individuals pay $2,000 per year to be members of the CNP. For $5,000, one can become a member of the Council's board of governors, which elects the executive committee of the CNP.

Some of the more well-known board members of the CNP include the Reverend Jerry Falwell, the leader of the now-defunct Moral Majority; Phyllis Schlafly, a leading anti-feminist; the Reverend Pat Robertson, right-wing TV evangelist; and Joseph Coors, whose family finances an interlocking network of ultra-conservative and far-right institutions. In 1983, the CNP bestowed their Thomas Jefferson Award to Senator Jesse Helms.

The lesser-known members of the CNP, like Batchelder, perhaps give better insight into the organization's politics:

- Richard Shoff, a former Ku Klux Klan leader in Indiana.
- John McGoff, a supporter of the former apartheid South African government.
- David Noebel, author of *Rhythm, Riots and Revolution*, a '60s book that attempted to show that folk music was a Communist plot.
- R.J. Rushdoony, the theological leader of America's "Christian Reconstruction" movement that advocates that Christian fundamentalists take "dominion" over America, abolish democracy, and institute Old Testament law. "Homosexuals...adulterers, blasphemers, astrologers and others will be executed," as well as disobedient children.
- Reed Larson, head of the anti-union National Right to Work Committee.
- Don Wildmon, TV censorship activist and accused anti-Semite.

Bellant specializes in the difficult task of tracking the historical roots of far-right groups. In his last book he noted: "The Council's creation was inspired by business and political leaders who are also leaders of the John Birch Society." This, in Bellant's analysis, is an important factor since it places the CNP not within the boundaries of mainstream conservative thought or traditional Republican Party ideals, but within the anti-democratic nativist tradition in American politics. The John Birch Society, for example, saw President Dwight Eisenhower as part of the international Communist conspiracy.

The Birch Society and the CNP have been intertwined since the Council's inception in 1981, when Tim LaHaye, a Moral Majority leader, received backing from Texas billionaire Nelson Bunker Hunt, a member of the Birch Society's National Council. By 1984, both John Birch Society Chairman A. Clifford Baker and Executive Council member William Cies were CNP members.

According to Bellant, "Five board members of Western Goals, essentially a JBS intelligence-gathering operation, joined the CNP as well." It was later revealed during the Iran-Contra scandal that Western Goals was used to funnel aid to the right-wing Contra guerrillas.

In 1982, Tom Ellis succeeded LaHaye as CNP president. Ellis was a director of the Pioneer Fund, a foundation that finances efforts to prove that African-Americans are genetically inferior to whites. Recipients of Pioneer Grants have included eugenicists William Shockley, Arthur Jensen and Roger Pearson. Pearson is on record advocating that "inferior races" should be "exterminated."

The John Birch Society, founded in 1958, was initially identified by scholars as a racist and anti-Semitic organization. The JBS spent much of its time in the '60s organizing against Martin Luther King Jr. and the civil rights movement. They accused King and civil rights activists of being Communist-controlled.

While the Birchers are regarded as extremists, both Bellant and Berlet warn that the CNPers like Batchelder are accepted as mainstream Republican Party leaders despite the company they keep.

April 2, 1997

White Power

How does the local daily newspaper cover the retirement of a "stalwart conservative" state representative? By overlooking ties to white supremacist groups, of course. The December 20, 1998, *Columbus Dispatch* featured a section-front story covering the retirement of House Speaker Pro-Tem William G. Batchelder, a Republican from Medina. The article, written by *Dispatch* Statehouse reporter Lee Leonard, described Batchelder as "a rock-ribbed conservative."

Leonard followed the next day with a laudatory Forum piece on Batchelder's retirement as the second most powerful man in the Ohio House. In Leonard's analysis, "Batchelder longed to be Speaker of the Ohio House and might have been, except that he refused to exchange his conservative principles for today's go-along practical politics." Leonard's articles are vague on the specifics of Batchelder's vaulted "conservative instincts."

Leonard ended his opinion piece by quoting Republican House Majority Leader Randall Gardner, who claimed, "There are few people who can't be replaced. Bill Batchelder is one of them."

Leonard's article and Forum opinion piece failed to mention that in April 1997, *Columbus Alive* revealed that Batchelder was listed as a member of a little-known and highly secretive far-right Council for National Policy (CNP). Author and investigative reporter Russ Bellant and Chip Berlet of Political

Research Associates both told *Alive* that the CNP had ties to white supremacists.

Similarly, the *Washington Post* reported on December 11 that one of President Bill Clinton's most ardent foes, Republican Representative Robert L. Barr Jr. of Georgia, acknowledged that he had given the keynote address earlier this year at the Council of Conservative Citizens (CCC) national board meeting. The CCC has a racist and anti-Semitic agenda similar to the CNP.

"Take 10 bottles of milk to represent all humans on Earth. Nine of them will be chocolate and only one white. Now, mix all those bottles together and you've gotten rid of the troublesome bottle of white milk. There too is the way to get rid of the world of whites. Convince them to mix their few genes with the genes of the many. Genocide via the bedroom chamber is as long lasting as genocide via war," reads a paragraph on a CCC website.

Barr, an ardent supporter of President Clinton's impeachment, recently said, "I came to the conclusion long ago that this President has brought disgrace to the office of the presidency and that something had to be done."

Batchelder, after 30 years in the Ohio House, will become a Medina County judge.

December 24, 1998

Right Wing Specter

So George W. Bush wants Pat Buchanan to stay in the Republican Party instead of bolting to the Reform Party and its $12 million "pot of gold" in matching funds. Why? Because, Bush says, "I need every vote I can get." Better a far-right Nazi apologist like Buchanan pissing out of the big Republican tent on Democrats than pissing in on Republicans.

I understand perfectly that Bush doesn't want to alienate the Holocaust deniers, crypto-fascists and the all-important gay-bashers vote clustered around Buchanan. The dirty little secret of the Republican Party in Ohio and nationally during the Reagan-Bush years is the GOP's established ties to various old-time fascists through its ethnic-outreach program. Russ Bellant's *Old Nazis, the New Right and the Republican Party* and Martin Lee's *The Beast Awakens* are both fine sources on this topic. Bellant wrote about ties between then-Governor, now U.S. Senator, George Voinovich and former Eastern European fascist immigrants.

The Buchanan record is easier to document for those who care. As White House Communication Director under Reagan, Buchanan regularly assailed the Justice Department's Office of Special Investigations (OSI), an agency established during the Carter years to find and prosecute Nazis and fascists who had entered the United States illegally. Buchanan is on record as an admirer of the deceased fascist dictator Franco, the Chilean butcher Pinochet and the former South African apartheid regime.

During the Reagan administration, Buchanan equated the Allies' treatment of German citizens after World War II to the Nazi's treatment of the Jews—an absurd claim favored by German and American neo-Nazis. Reportedly, Buchanan scripted Reagan's infamous and shocking remarks when he proclaimed buried SS soldiers at Bitburg "victims, just as surely as the victims in the concentration camps." The rock group the Ramones immortalized Reagan's words, and his bizarre comparison between the executioners and the executed, in their song "Bonzo Goes To Bitburg."

Buchanan believes Hitler was "an individual of great courage, a soldier's soldier," a line usually advanced by neo-Nazi and anti-Semitic publications like the *Spotlight* and the *Institute for Historical Review Journal*. Expect Pat's new tome, *A Republic, Not An Empire*, that offers the thesis that Hitler was eminently appeasable, to get favorable reviews in neo-Nazi circles. Also recall during the Reagan presidency, his Department of Education rejected a proposed Holocaust curriculum for federal funding because "the Nazi point of view, however unpopular, [was] not presented, nor [was] that of the Ku Klux Klan."

Both France's right-wing National Front leader Jean-Marie Le Pen and Pat Buchanan masqueraded as free market Reaganomic fanatics during the 1980s. After faithfully serving Reagan, Buchanan changed his tune during his 1992 bid for the Republican presidential nomination. Buchanan's program strongly mirrored the right-wing national populism of France's National Front. By appealing to everyone from the Christian Identity to the Christian Coalition and socially conservative Catholics, Buchanan's campaign allowed for the cross-fertilization of ideas between white supremacists and their less-overtly racist, but far more numerous, religious right allies. Hatred of gays, bashing of immigrants, opposition to abortion and fear of the mysterious "New World Order" brought them together in the Buchanan brigades.

Buchanan actually used the term "culture wars" during his speech before the Republican convention, the same phrase used by Nazis in the 1930s. He openly appealed to the Christian right with calculated phrases like "our culture is superior to other cultures, superior because our religion is Christianity."

As Arianna Huffington pointed out, in November 1998 Buchanan charged, "Non-Jewish whites—75 percent of the U.S. population—get just 25 percent of the slots...Now we know who's really getting the shaft at Harvard: white Christians." During the Reagan years, Buchanan argued against racial and ethnic quotas and insisted that people should be admitted to colleges based on merit. Now he's hinting at the pre-World War II anti-Jewish quota system prominent in elite universities.

Not only was Buchanan endorsed by several prominent religious-right leaders, but the anti-Semitic *Spotlight*, published by the Liberty Lobby, noted that, "Buchanan's campaign platform reads like nothing less than a statement of the Liberty Lobby's positions on the issues."

In 1996, Larry Pratt served as Buchanan's presidential campaign co-chairman. Pratt heads Gun Owners of America, but more important, is a key figure in American militia circles. Pratt attended the infamous October 1992 militia planning session in Colorado hosted by the notorious racist Christian Identity pastor Pete Peters. Pratt has shared the stage at rallies with Aryan Nation Chief Richard Butler and former KKK leader and guerrilla warfare specialist Louis Beam. Pratt resigned after the media exposed his ties to the neo-Nazi and white supremacist fringe.

Part of Buchanan's appeal, like the Nazis in the 1930s, is populist economics. His willingness to scapegoat immigrants to appease the financial insecurities of the average U.S. citizen left out of the 1990s economic boom fills a void created when President Bill Clinton led the "New Democrats" to the economic center.

But as long as local major party candidates ignore the everyday plight of workers, the specter of a right-wing national third party under Buchanan's control will continue to haunt us.

September 30, 1999

Strange Encounter With The Klan

Saturday in the park, I think it was the third of April. As the 110 or so assorted activists and hardcore anti-Klan fighters gathered at Whetstone Park at 10:30 in the morning, you knew it would be a weird scene in Coshocton.

"Mac" passed out maps and some last second advice—"Keep with friends, the Klan slime will attack if you stray"—while I rounded up *Democratic Left* producer Suzanne Patzer and computer guru Jim Laird and headed for the People's Liberation van. Jim handed me the Peacenet information on the Coshocton Klan rally. As I perused it, I thought about the history of the Klan.

The original Klan festered and grew in the aftermath of the Civil War. Essentially a secret organization of former Confederate army officers, the Klan was dedicated to the proposition that all blacks are born unequal.

The recent growth of the Klan can be tied directly to the Reagan and Bush years. After all, it was one of the Grand Wizards who noted that 1980 Republican platform "looked like it was written by a Klansman."

The Klan endorsed Reagan in 1980 and he, of course, rejected it. But not before Reagan appeared in New Philadelphia, Mississippi—the birthplace of the original

Klan—and told the good white people there that he, too, believed in "state's rights."

George Bush Sr. sent the new Klan a Valentine in the form of the Willie Horton TV commercial, signifying that even a New England preppie knew that most black men had nothing more than the rape of white women on their minds.

Jim's computer reconnaissance revealed little. It seems the Reverend Cliff N. Biggers had invited us to a "prayer service" at Shiloh Baptist Church in Coshocton, a small town east of Columbus, nestled in the rolling rural no-man's-land of east-central Ohio. Something called the Coshocton Community Coalition and the Coshocton Peacemakers Project welcomed "anti-Klan demonstrators."

They requested that we "voice our opposition to the Klan peacefully" and informed us that "peace activists from the Ready Response team from Athens, Ohio" were there to train us as "non-violent peacekeepers."

The Coalition also invited us to Coshocton Lake Park to express a "positive message of interracial community spirit" at a family picnic. They enticed us with "free hot dogs, soft drinks and activities for young people" including "clowns, games and fishing."

We never made it to the picnic, but we found the clowns.

When we arrived at Coshocton's courthouse grounds that afternoon, they were there: Seven bozos in white and black sheets with hoods, facing a thousand anti-Klan demonstrators mobilized to meet their match.

The first thing that struck me, although I'm a tried-and-true civil libertarian, is that the anti-Klan demonstrators ought to have allowed the Klan to march unimpeded in exchange for a law that requires them to wear bright red clown noses that honk.

Someone from the Coalition slipped me a note. It read: "The whole world is watching! We'll all be on tonight's news. If we attack the Klan, (verbally or physically) the Klan appears victim. Which group will then appear as the 'hate group'?" A thoughtful question, but most of the crowd was not in a very reflective mood.

The Klan, decked out in the mandatory white attire, was waving the stars and bars and bearing a cross. Chris Conners, the Grand Wizard—or Poobah, I forget which—from Bowling Green, Kentucky, was decked out in his best white robe with green trimmings. I caught him muttering something into the mike about "faggots and queers." I wasn't exactly sure if he was referring to his relationship with Calvin Reese, the only official Klansman in Coshocton, or simply being homophobic.

The crowd's first chant swelled from the direction of the Skinheads Against Racial Prejudice (SHARP). It went something like this: "You better watch out, we're going to fuck you up, the KKK, you know what's up."

The old Blue Oyster Cult refrain popped into my head: "This ain't the garden of Eden and there ain't no heaven above. Things ain't what they used to be, and this ain't the summer of love."

The next chant followed: "Hey, hey, ho, ho, fascist pigs have got to go, hey, hey, ho, ho…"

Mac explained to us why he'd helped organize the Columbus contingent, numbering between 150 and 200 people, to come to Coshocton. These people are dangerous, they come in contact with a lot of young people. There's a lot of young people here that came to hang out with the Klan, and they'll recruit their friends and become part of a movement. Anti-Klan activists provide an alternative voice at Klan rallies, giving kids a chance to listen to reason even as the Klan tries to fill their heads with hate.

"There's already a small group in Worthington High School and a small group at Westerville High School," Mac said. Both schools are in relatively affluent Columbus suburbs. "They're not very big. It only takes two or three of them to hurt people. I think the most effective thing here is to interfere with their ability to recruit new young members."

We approached three young Coshocton types to test Mac's thesis. One said, "I ain't allowed over here," meaning the area set aside for anti-Klan activists. But they referred us to their mentor, a middle-aged Coshocton man, for comment. In his assessment, the counter-demonstrators were all "queers on welfare." He wondered, "Why are there so many blacks here? They know they can't join." His young friends giggled.

Students from Kenyon College showed up in force. Forsaking the chants, they let their banners voice their opinions: "Difference is Our Strength." "My Race is Human." "The Time for Hate is Over." Alas, the obvious signs of dangerous "multiculturalism."

As the Grand Dragon babbled, taunting the crowd with an Arsenio Hall "woo-woo!" and discoursing on the need for blacks to put "Crisco oil" on their hair, the first signs of violence emerged. A SHARPy, who had spent too much time smashing racism and not enough time getting his arm in shape for baseball season, lobbed a large, economy-sized bottle toward the Klan. It fell short, smashing into the skull of a frontline anti-Klan protester.

As the Wizard advised everyone to "buy Coca-Cola," the frontline Klan fighters chanted, "Stop the attacks on the working class, kick the Klan in the ass." The chanting continued:

"Anti-union, anti-gay, fascist pigs, go away!"

One unidentified female Klan sympathizer, who would make her presence known later, loudly proclaimed, "You can't fuckin' hear nothin'." She seemed to be dismayed that she couldn't hear the words of the first Klanswoman to speak.

Wearing a Confederate flag as a bandanna and looking surprisingly like a redneck version of Mama Cass, I could only make out a few of her words over the howl of the crowd. She screamed: "We need to stand together! White is right! What about white pride?!"

Klansmen looked on with pride as she continued to puff her cigarette throughout her tirade. A Coshocton woman, who looked similar, repeatedly flipped the Klanswoman the bird and shouted, "Bitch! Bitch!"

The cops looked on. The growing line of county sheriffs stood pensively, but quickly leaped into action to make their first arrest as an anti-Klan protester leaned over the yellow police ribbon and refused to back up. As he was carted off to the Coshocton hoosegow, he surely heard the chant, "Let him go! Let him go!" And he no doubt heard: "The cops and the Klan go hand in hand, the cops and the Klan go hand in hand..."

"Scum in sheets, get off our streets! You in blue, you can go too..." The rhetoric was escalating, and so was the video war.

The Klan was videoing the protestors. The protesters were videoing the Klan. And the police were videoing everyone, including themselves. The ever-growing horde of blue-and-black-clad cops loomed large on the courthouse lawn. No one could miss the club-wielding, mounted police on large anti-riot horses moving to protect the Klan.

"Racists, sexist, anti-gay, fascist pigs, go away…"

As the moment to march grew near, the protestors challenged, "C'mon, just try it, fuck with us, we'll start a riot..." The frontline anti-fascist forces seemed sincere.

Suddenly, the seven Klansmen bolted towards the street protected by a regiment of approximately 175 rural sheriff's deputies, and what seemed like a traditional seventh Calvary unit. The counter-protestors moved just as quickly to engulf the parade.

"Move, move, move! Go, go, go," the protestors advised one another. The distinctive voice of a TV news reporter floated overhead. The baritone intoned, "The crowd is moving exuberantly...."

The Klan now controlled the street. All seven of them. And they were hell-bent on holding it with the aid of the cops. The first sounds of launched projectiles echoed amidst cries of "Rock that bitch!" "Rock that bitch" gave way to a singular chant, "Death, death, death to the Klan!"

Wisely decked out in my black high-top Nike "felony flyers," I raced with the videocamera to record the street scene. The rest of the *Democratic Left* crew followed in hot pursuit. The police were determined to hold the street. Everyone was ordered to the sidewalk, even my video crew. But not without a minor confrontation with the forces of law and order.

We told them we were with public access television. The officer on horseback said, "It doesn't matter." Suzanne, in standard progressive attire, worked at spin control: "We're with the parade. We're marching with the Klan." The police weren't buying it. As the large horse cornered us against an automobile, the police seemed to have won the argument.

It seemed, as Yogi Berra liked to say, like "déjà vu all over again." There were Confederate banners in the street. Ugly police attack dogs. Police with clubs and horses. Was it the '60s? Were we in Birmingham? Was that Sheriff Bull Connor ahead with a megaphone?

I feared arrest for trying to record this small bit of history. Suzanne, unsympathetically advised, "If they arrest you give me the camera!" Arrest me for what? Videotaping without blow-dried hair? The police frantically chased a reported 16-year-old, who they suspected of rock throwing with "extreme malice." An officer on foot finally cornered her against the building with the help of a cop riding Fury or Flicka.

They let her go after she chanted, "I didn't throw shit! I didn't throw shit!" The cop on foot confided, "I hate this job." Another on horseback seemed to relish his sworn duty somewhat more as he galloped his horse up on the sidewalk, panicking the protestors.

A woman lay in the street bleeding from the head, a cop stood over her with a club. The police would later officially report she was hit by a rock. That's not how the protestors saw it as they scattered before the thundering hooves.

It had been a long, strange trip around the block with the Klan. An anonymous protester commented, "Some of that shit back there reminded me of that Rodney King situation." Was Rodney King hit with rocks too?

Meanwhile, back at the courthouse someone lobbed a chunk of metal at the Klan, which missed its intended mark and shattered the glass door of the building. Mama Cass looked worried.

The police swarmed into the crowd to arrest a female student from Antioch College alleged to be responsible for the shattered glass. They also choked our camerawoman, who attempted to videotape the arrest. "What law was I breaking? Would you do that to Channel 6 news?" A reasonable query under the circumstances.

Finally the Klan gave in as the police fought to control the courthouse turf. The Klan displayed their traditional bravery and requested protective custody from the police. An official-looking sheriff-type grabbed a megaphone and addressed the crowd, his words drowned in wave after wave of crowd chants. Maybe he was ordering people to disperse, maybe he was inviting us to visit Coshocton Lake Park—who knows?

Another officer told the crowd to go home. Somebody responded it wasn't over until the Klan went home. Another voice added, "It's not over 'til the fascist bullshit's gone!"

I moved to the frontline and borrowed a megaphone. My journalistic skills honed, I tried to interview Calvin Reese, Mr. Klan in Coshocton. I brought up the question of his wife being bi-racial. The interviewee was not responsive. But a friend of his, the Klan sympathizer we spoke of earlier, did respond by hocking a big loogey in the direction of our camera crew and inadvertently toward former *Free Press* publisher Duane Jager. Klanswomen can be so enticing when they're riled.

As the cops ushered the Klan away, the vast majority of the crowd drifted toward their vehicles. A small, hardcore group stayed on the courthouse lawn and played dodge the big horses as well as reminisce about the day's activities. I have a flashback of jumping over a bush and almost landing on Rin-Tin-Tin to avoid a very large hoofed creature.

Some of the strangest happenings of the day occurred in the rally's aftermath. About 50 anti-Klan protestors decided they would march to the police station and demand the release of their friends and comrades. The Coshocton sheriff would later describe them as "a riotous mob bent on a jailbreak."

The protestors obviously didn't know they were a mob, and nobody informed them of their plans to take over the Coshocton jail. Our video crew thought we'd tag along and get the names of the arrested at the police station. The mounted police had other ideas.

We approached the police with a friendly and simple question, "Which way is the police station?" So frightened by the riotous gang of three from Columbus, obvious public access maniacs and alternative journalist types, the police responded by charging their horses into us.

The camerawoman's pleas of "Wait, wait, wait..." did little to dissuade the police from dancing the bump with her. The horses had no rhythm. The police, emboldened by their crushing of an obvious criminal media conspiracy, decided to practice mounted-horse crowd dispersing tactics. Rewriting the Constitution, they were determined to clear the park. No citizen could be on the courthouse property, and they had the horses to enforce it.

They drove the scattered remnants of the anti-Klan forces to the edge of the street. A woman from Coshocton, as she backed up, explained why it was a strategic retreat: "Well, they hit a girl over here and sliced her head wide open. She was just standing there." Clearly the police had not informed her that she'd been officially hit by a rock.

My riotous co-conspirators and I took a final stand on the edge of the street against the seventh cavalry. I demanded they explain under what law they were dispersing peaceful protestors. Grasping for the only social authority I could think of, I told them I was the co-publisher of the *Free Press* and, as a citizen and possessor of freedom of speech, I challenged them: "If you want to take on the First Amendment, take it on!"

The remnant non-rioters cheered. I demanded that the modern version of General Custer, who had just defended the Klan, now defend my rights. He responded quite professionally, "We're trying to do that, sir." But the protesters had the final word. Spontaneously, and in one voice, they shouted, "Bullshit!"

It was Saturday in Coshocton. I think it was the third of April. We headed back to the People's Liberation van, walking over a sign that read, "Real Men Don't Wear Sheets." Nor perhaps, do they wield clubs on horseback.

Columbus Free Press
May 1993

When The Klan
Kame To Kolumbus

Well the Klan finally came to Columbus. Their October 23 rally produced three obvious observations: The KKK pretty much talked to themselves at taxpayer's expense; despite an intensive PR campaign, the downtown power structure and city officials could not keep counter-demonstrators away from the event; and the younger "Generation X" anti-Klan protestors displayed a new level of militancy and rage.

Only an overwhelming police presence—at least 500 cops—and expensive and extreme security measures preserved the Klan's ability to speak. Marchers were directed along "official routes" and subjected to metal-detector searches prior to entering the fenced-in anti-Klan containment area. On the other side of the fence stood a massive police phalanx protecting the Klan as they propagandized behind still another security fence.

There was consensus among mainstream media types that we would never learn the exact cost of protecting the Klan. People talked of a betting pool, predicting how many budgets the costs would be buried in.

Let's see, overtime for 500 highly trained police officers, the new fences, the scaffolding, the resulting round-the-clock construction, the massive police surveillance, communications command posts set up in the high-rise across from the Statehouse, the helicopters and, of course, well over a month of secret and not-so-secret police attendance at anti-Klan organizational meetings. Add the cost of the police junket to Indianapolis for training, and the mind reels.

Jim McNamara, local attorney and anti-Klan activist, called it "a million-dollar press conference for the Klan." The mainstream press seemed to settle on a $250,000 figure (at least privately). From their fortress enclave on the Statehouse steps, the two dozen thoroughly modern Klansmen—sans robes, sunglasses replacing hoods, preaching "love" of white folks while singling out "queers" over "Negroes"—preened for the cameras, giving a Sieg Heil-type salute as cued.

This is the new, high-tech, Euro-looking Klan: *GQ* white supremacy. They're not interested in their granddaddy's white-trash Klan.

They may have been "sharping" and "stylin'" in their new robes, but their followers missed the fashion show. Only six pro-Klan supporters briefly, very briefly, mingled with the 2,000 anti-Klan demonstrators. One white supremacist couple, identifying themselves as Russ and Lisa, found themselves in police protective custody along with four visibly shaken neo-Nazi youth. One Sieg Heil-ed his crotch to cover the pee stain.

Russ lost his prized Confederate bandanna to overwhelming hostile forces, promising him unity with their fists unless he gave it up. "I'm not pro-Klan, I just think states should be allowed to have their own flag if they want it," explained Russ. "I tell black people, they've got their X, and I've got my X on the Confederate flag."

Lisa was a little bolder. "I support the Klan, and I'm not scared," she said. Russ looked pained as his bandanna was set ablaze to the chant of "Burn, baby, burn!"

Russ, Lisa, and their four white supremacist cohorts were escorted out before they could hear the words of Klansman Thom Robb. No other pro-Klan individuals asserted their presence during the rally.

"The Klan has no real following, that's the story," according to Bob Handelman, local attorney and long-time Klan foe. Indeed, Klan fever seemed extremely non-contagious in Columbus.

McNamara declared the counter-demonstration a great success. He noted, "I don't think they recruited one new member today, and they may have lost a few. That's why we organize to confront them."

Unfortunately, they still may have turned it into a recruitment opportunity. The Klan's banner contained no slogan, only its name and post office box, which was flashed on TV screens across the nation: A free how-to-contact the Klan ad for anybody who was too intimidated to come downtown. Of course, there's nothing to stop anti-Klan protestors from flooding the P.O. box with cards and letters.

If there were any obvious government failures during the Klan rally, it was the mayor's inability to keep large numbers of anti-Klan protestors away from the site. The repeated police warnings that the police couldn't "guarantee" the public's safety at the rally were sneered at by activist Barry Edney. "Hell, they've never been worried about my safety before," he said, "it's the Klan's safety they can't guarantee."

The *Columbus Dispatch* termed the anti-Klan turnout smaller than expected, but the daily paper ran photos of the demonstrators and the officially sanctioned Unity Day crowds side-by-side, providing graphic documentation that the protestors at the Statehouse out-numbered the hug-a-thon crowd at Ohio State by at least four to one.

As the officially orchestrated Unity Day procession proceeded according to script on the OSU campus, Mark Welsh, of the Native American Indian Center, pondered, "Why doesn't that Community Relations Commission investigate that 300-foot statue of a racist headed for our city?" referencing the Russian-made Christopher Columbus statue sought after by city leaders. Well, what else could a world-class city with a replica of the Santa Maria on its riverfront yearn for?

The mayor's first-time utilization of the so-called Community Relations Commission (CRC)—an organization established in the wake of the Rodney King and local Oleatha Waugh police beatings—seemed not only disingenuous, but surreal. During the weeks leading up to the Klan rally, members of the CRC invaded various anti-Klan organizational meetings and pleaded for young activists to attend Unity Day events. Police, both uniformed and plain-clothed, also attended the anti-Klan meetings, claiming they were there to assist the organizers with their protesting needs.

With the mayor denouncing the demonstrators, this struck most as odd. But, hey, who knows what the cops are thinking? With the Republican Mayor Greg Lashutka presiding, Unity Day elevated local political hypocrisy to new heights.

Anti-Klan activists repeatedly charged that Lashutka condoned the overtly racist electoral strategies of the Reagan-Bush years. They pointed out that the 1980 Republican platform was endorsed by the KKK; Reagan kicked off his campaign in New Philadelphia, Mississippi, birthplace of the Klan, and said he supported "states' rights"; he granted Bob Jones University tax-exempt status while the school practiced apartheid in the name of Jesus; and that Bush scared the hell out of white suburbanites with his Willie Horton commercial.

And where was Greg Lashutka when all this was happening?

Kissing Bush's and Reagan's behind.

Handelman recalled that Lashutka was the point man for Supreme Court nominee Robert Bork in central Ohio. "He supported Bork for the Supreme Court, a man who argues the 'original intent' doctrine, a man who believes that states should be able to discriminate against Jews, blacks and gays. Give me a break. Unity Day?"

A local AFSCME staffer pointed out that Lashutka was currently in the process of privatizing the city's sanitation department, historically the source of decent-paying jobs for minorities and inner-city residents: "He should be forced to explain at Unity Day how he is going to destroy civil service jobs and give sweetheart deals to his rich, white suburban friends."

Not only did the counter-demonstrators come in large numbers to protest the Klan, they demonstrated a new spirit of militancy and, some of them, a frightening amount of pure rage. They attempted, despite the massive police presence, to tear down the security fence protecting the Klan. And they were Maced.

New groups like the National Women's Rights Organizing Committee and Love and Rage, an anarchist federation, displayed a fearless contempt for police authority. These groups, incubated in the urban ghettoes of New York, Detroit, and Cleveland during the devastating de-industrialization and urban blight of the Bush years, are determined to overthrow the status quo. Their attitudes and tactics picked up a few adherents even in the staid all-American test market of Columbus.

Indigenous militant organizations, like Columbus' Ordinary People's Movement, will soon be looked on as voices of responsible moderation if these outside groups grow amidst the poverty and despair of the central city. Edney, spokesperson for the Ordinary People's, made it clear that he favored "confrontation, not violence" with the Klan. His organization, marching from the Near East Side, proved quite successful in organizing and policing their own members.

Still, when the Klan had finally retreated, and the demonstrators began to disperse, there was a miniscule but menacing minority of African-American youth who wanted not only to fight the police but the white anti-Klan protestors as well. Steeped in "gangsta" rap and absolute rage, distrusting all formal institutions, they sought to provoke violence.

"I'm going to fuck all the white bitches I can 'cause I hate them," one said.

"Spend a million dollars defending the Klan and my car's broke down and I can't get a job. What have you ever done for me?" another asked a white passerby.

Some threatened to "kick all white ass" as soon as the cops left. This is a small but growing sentiment in urban America. The multicultural united front carried the day at the Statehouse—the true "unity day" rally. But the forces of radicalism, anarchism and pure nihilism fester daily. As the riots of South Central L.A. demonstrated, what does the urban underclass really have to lose if they tear down the system and start all over again?

I was reminded of this as I retreated for a cup of coffee on High Street after the rally. Behind the shop I saw a genuine but pathetic display of racial unity: a black man and a white man cooperating in their quest for food in the garbage bins of the All-American city, Columbus.

Columbus Free Press
November 1993

Radical Rebirth

Every 30 years or so, the American left recreates itself: The Communists and Socialists of the 1930s "Red Decade" later became the decentralized, radical Students for a Democratic Society and New Left of the 1960s. And it looks like it's the multiculturalism and direct action of Anti-Racist Action (ARA) for the '90s.

The program for the ARA's Third Annual Conference in 1996 screamed: "Do Something!" It had a photo of an activist taking a swing at a bloated, pot-bellied, berobed, coneheaded Klansman. Entering the old North High School in Columbus, where the ARA conference was held, I got the sense that something was indeed happening here. Grizzled veterans of '60s and '70s anti-war and anti-imperialist movements mingled freely with the next New Left. Before the weekend was over, I had attended workshops on racism and fascism, marched and been Maced at—and been cited as the leader of—a demonstration against police brutality. Welcome to activism, '90s style.

At the opening of the conference Friday night, the mostly "straight-edge" Generation X participants—wearing "Fuck Racism" T-shirts, the "Mean People Suck" slogan taken to its logical extreme—exuded an aura that made the Weathermen look like the Brady Brunch. But, how much was posing and posturing? This new generation of anti-racist militants has

179

grown up knowing no victories. The Civil Rights movement—which brought the end of legalized apartheid in America in 1965—is ancient history. The anti-war struggle is like those war stories that the World War II GIs used to tell their kids and grandkids in the '50s.

This new breed of activists has done battle in the cities, suburbs and small towns of North America against the rising tide of neo-fascists and neo-Nazis ushered in by the rhetoric of the Reagan and Bush eras and the infamous political "wedge issues" of immigrant and welfare-mother bashing, a tide not quelled by the hollow promises of President Clinton's law-and-order-centrist policies.

And this is true not only for the Americans present, but for the large Canadian contingent as well. The dozens of ARA members from Toronto are hardened by their ongoing battle with white supremacists in the Great White North. Toronto is the home of Ernest Zundel, a key player in the international Nazi movement. From his fortress at 206 Carlton, Zundel runs Samisdat Publishing, one of the largest Nazi propaganda operations on the planet. His chief goal is to deny the Holocaust, producing such publications as: "Did Six Million Really Die?" and "The Hitler We Loved And Why."

Canadian courts have dismissed Holocaust denial charges against Zundel, instead characterizing his work as concerning "ethnic conflict between Germans and Jews." Yeah, and those death camp ovens were used for making bagels. Zundel's racist skinhead ("bonehead") followers revere him as a hero and chant, "Six million more!"

But when government action fails, this new breed of anti-fascist activist is willing to use other means: Zundel's property was recently torched.

Shedding light on the rise of the American religious right

on the conference's opening night was an old friend of mine from Detroit, Russ Bellant. His new book, *The Religious Right in Michigan Politics*, is the first to investigate and document the origins and objectives of the popular group the Promise Keepers (PK). Many are familiar with former University of Colorado football coach Bill McCartney's original 1990 vision: to fill a stadium with Christian men willing to "reclaim" authority from their wives, capitalizing on the male backlash against the women's movement and the gender-bashing so prominent now on talk radio.

As Bellant explained, the vast majority of men of various denominations that attend these PK rallies come with good and sincere intentions. I know—my older brother Nick and my younger brother Dave, both plagued by marital problems, now call themselves Promise Keepers.

Bellant pointed out how McCartney, while serving as assistant football coach at the University of Michigan at Ann Arbor, "encountered and was deeply influenced by the Word of God (WOG) Community." WOG, according to Bellant, practices a "shepherding/discipleship" form of worship that requires total submission to a person called "the head." He calls Promise Keepers' views fundamentally "anti-democratic" and potentially "totalitarian" in nature.

"The use of sophisticated lighting and sound in a stadium setting, psychologically playing on people's emotions, breaking down the denominational differences and merging nationalism and religion really echoes the Nazi rallies of the Third Reich," Bellant argued. Bellant demonstrated how virtually all top Christian right leaders—Pat Robertson of the Christian Coalition, D. James Kennedy of Coral Ridge Ministry and Bill Bright of Campus Crusade for Christ—have signed on to the Promise Keepers. The "family values" rhetoric and homophobia are part of a larger "cultural revolution" the PKs hope to bring about. Robertson, Kennedy and Bright, along with James Dodson—the author of *Promise Keepers Manifesto, Seven Promises of a Promise Keeper*—are all members of the super-secretive radical right Council for National Policy (CNP), according to Bellant.

The CNP, created by business and political leaders who were also leaders in the John Birch Society, represents the political elite of the radical right and essentially plans and funds the major projects of the American right, in Bellant's analysis. The big bucks come from Jeff Coors and family members of Coors Brewing Company, Linda Bean of L.L. Bean, and Richard DeVos Jr. of Amway and Texas oilman Nelson Bunker Hunt.

"While they appeal to black members, their real agenda is to destroy affirmative action, and they have links to white supremacist ideology," Bellant concluded.

Activists attended ARA conference sessions like "Leonard Peltier/Political Prisoners," "Black-Jewish Relations," "Lesbian and Gay Oppression" and the essential "Surviving Radical Demos" to name a few. Having attended, participated, organized and covered literally hundreds of protests and demonstrations in my life, I thought I knew how to survive a radical demo in the mid '90s.

To err is human…

I was asked to bring my portable PA system to the conference at 6 p.m. Saturday for the "Copwatch Rally & March." No big deal, just another case of journalistic participant-observer in the alternative press. Soon I was wondering who was organizing the event. When I arrived at the kickoff point at Arcadia and High streets, security guru Chris "The Anarchist" handed me a mike and asked me to speak.

"About what?" I asked.

"You know, about why we're marching."

Luckily I was saved by a Columbus Copwatch member who politely asked the gathering horde of Klan and Nazi fighters "to remember that your actions will have repercussions on us in this community." Virtually all got the message: Give peace a chance tonight.

I briefly addressed the assembled. Having a Ph.D in political science, I knew to announce the intent of the march to the estimated 10 percent that were no doubt undercover cops: "We intend this march to be a lawful demonstration, to protest police brutality and walk the streets of America without fear of the police..." I said more about the Antioch College students being beaten at the federal building, and Channel 4's TV footage showing the brutalization of students on 12th Avenue, but my main mission had been accomplished: protecting myself from "inciting a riot" charges. Wise move.

A small contingent of anarchists from the "Love and Rage" group unfurled a red-and-black flag. Banners were held with slogans reading "No Police Brutality" and "No Nazis, No Killer Cops, No Fascist USA, Anti-Racist Action." Appropriate slogans for the twentysomething generation whose educational benefits have been cut while government prison spending has been quadrupled.

Other marchers lit torches—lawful, but virtually unheard-of in Columbus—creating an eerie and disturbing mood. These weren't drunken frat boys reveling in a football victory frenzy. We crossed High Street and more than a hundred people began marching south.

Police squad cars with lights flashing immediately began to "escort" the marchers. They persisted, despite our insistence that we knew our way to 12th Avenue. And as a police helicopter began to hover overhead, I heard an unfamiliar chant: "Aim high, pigs in the sky!"

Just before Blake, in front of the Radio Shack and 24-hour video store, shit happened. Stuck hauling the PA system, I heard a scuffle and turned to see a weird scene. My mind at first rejected it: There was a female police officer without riot gear, attempting to arrest a male marcher. He had his hands raised out to his sides and she was screaming and pulling on his arm. Someone was pulling on his other arm, a literal tug-of-war. Someone in the crowd was yelling "Fuck the pigs!" Seems one Jason Robert Maffettone, 27, of Hoboken, New Jersey, had stepped off the curb in Columbus, "jaywalkers gulch." Omigod.

Officer Julie Appenzeller, sworn to serve and protect the people of Columbus from all jaywalkers, foreign and domestic, was just doing her job. Startled and disbelieving male officers stood by their gal as the crowd and I shouted "No police brutality! Let him go!"

The infamous "Have Mace—will spray you" Columbus cops drew their black cans. When you're chanting into a mike, you can't always pay attention when someone's aiming at your big round head. Just my luck. I met up with Officer Generic Cop, six-foot-one with black hair and a mustache, who of course finished first at the police academy in Mace target shooting. I didn't actually see the Mace; I felt it when it drenched my eyes. For 10 to 15 seconds I was really mad. This asshole clearly hadn't read the U.S. Constitution, nor Columbus police procedure on Macing. He'd flunk my American government class. Moot point as my eyes began to burn, lungs sear, and nose clog up. Still, chanting into a mike on a sidewalk does not constitute menacing a police officer.

Let's see, five minutes into an anti-police brutality march and I've been Maced. Go figure. I pride myself on never getting Maced. I hadn't been Maced since the day after the Klan killed civil rights marchers in Greensboro, North Carolina. My mind raced. When was that? 1979? '80? Anyway, it was probably tear gas. Or was it pepper gas at Kent State in '78?

Déjà vu all over again. I was on my knees choking and crawling, my Columbus tax dollars at work again. Being a brave journalist, I thought I'd best crawl into the video store to wash out my eyes. Luckily my alternative press fame had preceded me. The clerk greeted me with a cheery: "Hi Bob!" My coverage of the sheriff's efforts to shut down porn shops aside, it seems the only restroom was in the triple-X adult section of the store. Half-blinded but still able to make out the images of assorted sex toys, I made my way to the counter. "Bathroom," I pleaded. The clerk had seen it all before. "Honest, I've got Mace in my eyes. It's not a Pee Wee Herman thing."

He advised, "Just ride it out. The water will only make it worse." A voice of authority.

Outside, things had calmed down and I found myself at the end of the march. Fortunately, one young ARA activist was carrying a squirt tube of Bausch and Lomb sensitive eye contact lens cleaner. "It'll work, dude. Like, I sprayed myself with some Mace and tested it." It was like a miracle. No Columbus activist should leave home without it.

Freed of the speaker system, now safely stashed at an ARA safe house on High Street thanks to Chris "The Anarchist," I moved to the front of the march. There I met 30 or so police in riot gear, and reporters from the *Columbus Dispatch*, Channel 4 and Channel 10.

I had a new goal. Keep from getting Maced again. Tensions mounted as the marchers, now swelled to nearly 300, found themselves pinned against a construction fence in the middle of the campus. Would the police attack?

Undoubtedly, they were wondering the same about us. Instead of confronting the police, we found an opening at the Wexner Center and snaked through the campus. Thank God for secular humanist bastions of liberalism. One lone campus police car escorted us several blocks back to High Street. We figured the campus cops were unlikely to Mace us, but they might order us to do a big group hug.

The moment of truth: Should we walk down 12th Avenue? What the hell, it's still America, why not? The march ended almost without incident as we re-emerged at 15th and High and gathered in the open space in front of the Wexner Center.

Just before the end of the march, a lone police commander joined the marchers. The word went out that he was looking for Fitrakis. No doubt, I thought, to congratulate me for my fine work in averting a riot. Wrong again. The first tip off was when he wouldn't shake my hand. And then his first words stung like the Mace: "I'm Commander Marcum. Why are you writing those lies about me?"

How the hell was I to know he'd been reassigned from supervisor of Police Intelligence to riot patrol at OSU? And anyway, those tips about his family's links to gambling were from my most reliable law-enforcement sources. I asked him what the real story was, but he wouldn't tell me. "Your paper's printing lies." Later that night the police reported that no Mace was used on the demonstrators.

The next day's *Dispatch* reported that I "led" the rally. I didn't mean to, but as my old marching buddy Mark Stansbery explained it, "There really was no leadership. And after Bob got Maced, he was really pissed."

The ARA doesn't really have leaders. It's a new movement of leaderless resistance to police brutality and the prison-industrial complex.

The *Dispatch* also reported the post-Macing chant as: "Police brutality, we're sick and...tired of it." Insert "fuckin'" where the ellipse is. That's the mood of these young ARA activists. America is incubating a whole new generation of hard-core fascist-fighters that are sick and tired. And tired of being sick and tired. They're not the Promise Keepers, but they are the product of America's broken promises and dreams.

October 23, 1996

Three Reichs
And You're Out

Whether it's in January around Martin Luther King Jr. Day or February during Black History Month, Columbus' yearly visit from hate-mongering white supremacists was once again counter-protested by the weather. From subzero wind chills to Alberta Clippers the last few years, it's almost enough to make one believe in divine intervention.

Harold "Ray" Redfearin, leader of Ohio's wing of the white terrorist Aryan Nations organization, is busy trying to unite all of the state's white supremacist groups under the umbrella of the misnamed Christian Identity theology. Redfearin's using the so-called Church of the Good Shepherd in New Vienna, Ohio, to spew his theology of hate. Christian Identity code phrases include the old canard that "the Jews are the spawn of Satan" and that blacks are "pre-Adamic," as in Adam and Eve, "mudpeople"—thus, not human.

About 40 white supremacists, including Redfearin and Troy Murphy, an imperial wizard of an Indiana Klan group, rallied at the Statehouse last Sunday, February 16, 1997. As usual, state, county and local police provided tough and overzealous security for the white supremacists. At 12:30 p.m., counter-demonstrators began gathering at the corner of Broad and High.

Hundreds of Anti-Racist Action (ARA) activists, primarily

from the Midwest and East Coast, swelled the ranks of the anti-Nazi protesters. The campus-area Food Not Bombs organization offered up vegetarian chili to the gathering throng. Barry Edney of the Ordinary People's Movement, who had organized the most noticeable African-American contingent, was whipping up the crowd until he strayed into some Nation of Islam rhetoric.

Police officers appear to have perfected their infamous counter-demonstrator harassment techniques. Crowd them together, make them pass through an X-ray gate, run metal detectors over them, search and frisk them before they can exercise their First Amendment right to heckle the Klan. Make no mistake about it, law enforcement officials have created a deliberate policy, under the guise of security, where only two metal-detecting gates are used to impede the rights of counter-demonstrators.

The police obsession with Nazi and Klan First Amendment rights is reaching new levels of absurdity, as is their disciplined practice of harassing counter-demonstrators. After waiting some 40 minutes just to get into the area, this writer was immediately thrown out by the Columbus SWAT team, reportedly under the supervision of Commander Curtis Marcum. My alleged offense was crossing over an imaginary line by a sign that said "EXIT."

Despite repeatedly identifying myself as a journalist for *Columbus Alive*, the entire SWAT unit guarding the exit seemed to take pleasure in ejecting me. Perhaps it was the articles I've written exposing the alleged gambling practices of the Marcum family at the gambling house run by the murdered ex-police officer Mt. Vernon Johnson that made me such a dangerous suspect. Having taken an imaginary step across the arbitrary invisible line, known only unto God and the SWAT team, I was immediately grabbed in a pressure hold on my wrist and told "You must exit." No, they weren't arresting me, they were evicting me. This must be the SWAT team's new training to "protect and serve."

Just before the exit, two apparent undercover officers, one male and one female in a fur coat—as always, sticking out like the proverbial sore thumb—were checking in with a Franklin County sheriff's officer. The woman turned to chime in: "Get him out of here! He's always causing trouble!"

The sheriff's deputy joined in: "Him again! Get him out of here!" So much for my First Amendment rights.

I re-entered after more police hassles and a less-than-friendly extra testicle squeeze during my re-frisking, just in time to see a burly biker being confronted by ARA activists. "That's an SS insignia on your jacket, you Nazi scum!" At first the biker tried to deny it, but fled quickly after someone kicked him in the butt. He was allowed to go out the entrance. Where was the SWAT team when you needed them?

As I approached the fence to take my first photo of the racist clan, I realized they were leaving. Less than an hour into their rally their vituperative diatribe was over. Perhaps they had counted too much on the spirits of Mussolini and Hitler rising from the pit of hell to inspire them. Or maybe they were scared off by a frightful vision of themselves strung up on a meathook in a public square or blowing their brains out in a godawful bunker.

The eternal post-World War II debate continued. What do you do with a nascent Nazi movement? "We tried ignoring them in Germany in the '20s and '30s," argued Jim McNamara, local ARA spokesperson. "This gives our organization an opportunity to educate people. We had a lot of energy out there. I was proud of the spirit of our activists. We stopped the

Nazis from recruiting and we got to recruit, communicate with our fellow citizens and leaflet a lot of neighborhoods in the name of interracial unity. I'd call that a success."

February 19, 1997

Buckeye Battle Cry

What the hell's happening in Ohio? The Kehoe brothers, Chevie and Cheyne, white supremacists, shoot it out with state troopers in Wilmington, Ohio; Aryan Nations, the American Nazi party, Klansmen, racist skinheads and Christian Identity hate preachers converge at the Statehouse; and Peter Langan, leader of the Midwest Bank Bandits and the Aryan Republican Army, is busted living on the south side of Columbus—here in the heart of it all.

White supremacists who've long dreamed of their "own private Idaho"—where Aryan Nations founder Richard Butler established his 20-acre compound in rural Hayden Lake in the early '70s—now have their sights set on Ohio.

Floyd Cochran, former high-ranking Aryan Nations official turned anti-racist activist, repeatedly warned that Ohio, especially the southeast portion, is a prime target of white supremacists. "Just last fall I spoke in Athens, Ohio, before a feminist group and I warned them of the growing danger in Ohio. The organizer told me that I should quit frightening people, that she lives in Ohio and I don't know what I'm talking about," recalled Cochran.

Unfortunately, Cochran knows all too well the dangers of Aryan Nations. He lives in Pennsylvania, close to Mark Thomas' farm outside Macungie. Thomas, who was indicted on January 30 as a co-conspirator in the Midwest Bank Bandit robberies, is a key link between American white supremacists organizations. Thomas has served as national leader of the violent anti-government Posse Comitatus, as "Imperial Chaplain" of the Invisible Empire Knights of the Ku Klux Klan, as a Christian Identity preacher and, until his recent indictment, the Aryan Nations' leader in Pennsylvania.

During the 1990s, Thomas attracted scores of skinheads and assorted white supremacists to rallies and weekly "Bible Studies" at his Macungie compound. Thomas' tactics revolve around creating a united front of racists and anti-Semites.

It should come as no shock that the Kehoe brothers from Colville, Washington, a short distance from Butler's Hayden Lake compound, shot it out with state troopers in Wilmington. They were, no doubt, in the area for the gathering of the racist tribes. Just 10 miles from Wilmington is New Vienna, where Ohio racists are dreaming of a white revolution and building for that day.

Anthony "Tony" Wayne Gamble, Imperial Wizard of the Knight Riders of the KKK, testified back in June 1995 in a case concerning the tearing down of the Klan cross in Cincinnati. He revealed how his Ross, Ohio-based Klan members worked with Aryan Nation supporters at the Christian Identity House of the Good Shepherd's church in New Vienna. This is where the Klan's Cincinnati Christmas cross was built in 1994.

This Klan/Nazi merger under the guise of white supremacist Christian Identity theology is pivotal to understanding the current racial violence in Ohio. As *Klanwatch* reported in March 1995, the more violent white supremacist group Aryan Nations staged an alarming comeback in 1994. In 1993, Aryan Nations was in only three states. Aided by money provided by the Midwest Bank Bandits, the Idaho-based group swept into 15 new states in 1994, including Ohio, and ended up in 30 states by 1995. Aryan Nations had declined dramatically after its peak in 1983-84, after its offshoot, the Order, killed a state trooper, an Aryan Nation member and Jewish talk show host Alan Berg. The Order, like the Midwest Bank Bandits, specialized in armed robberies to finance the racist revolution.

With the rise of the Aryan Nations in 1994, so rose militia and states' rights organizations in the aftermath of the 1992 Ruby Ridge, Idaho, shoot-out between the FBI and the white separatist Randy Weaver; and the destruction of the Waco, Texas Branch Davidian complex in 1993. Ohio saw the dramatic rise of the Ohio Unorganized Militia.

Michael Hill, chaplain in the Militia and an organizer of Ohio's One Supreme Court, a common-law court that meets regularly in Columbus, was shot to death during a traffic stop on June 28, 1995, in Muskingum County. The *Columbus Dispatch* reported that Michael Hill's widow, Arlene, held a memorial service for her slain husband on Sunday, June 30, 1995. It casually mentioned that Colorado preacher Pete Peters and North Carolinian Nord Davis "are scheduled to speak."

What it failed to mention was that Peters is one of America's more influential and active Christian Identity propagandists and theologians. His sermons are based on the militant Christian Identity and anti-Semitic beliefs that Jews pose a satanic threat to American civilization, that black and other people of color are subhuman and that homosexuals should be executed.

In Michael Barkham's book *Religion and the Racist Right*, he discusses Peters' Remnant Resolves—a statement of political principles concerning Identity believers. Peters holds that God's law is "binding...on all men, regardless of their political persuasion or personal beliefs." Thus, "the role of civil authority is to administer God's law." The logic of this belief is that secular humanist civil authorities, whether cops or judges, don't have to be obeyed. God's law, of course, is known only to the likes of Michael Hill, Pete Peters, Tony Gamble, Richard Butler, Mark Thomas and their racist ilk.

Nord Davis, the other speaker mentioned by the *Dispatch*, is a well-known North Carolina white supremacist who organized a trip to Jordan during the Gulf War to support Saddam Hussein. After all, it's standard Christian Identity doctrine that the Zionist Jews, the spawn of Satan, are spiraling history toward Armageddon. The presence of preeminent racists like Davis and Peters at Hill's memorial established all-too-clear links between the Ohio Unorganized Militia and the white supremacist movement.

The anti-government sentiments of the militia movement make it a prime recruiting ground for white supremacists. A May 1995 *Newsweek* article reported that federal investigators of the Oklahoma City bombing were "looking closely at a white supremacist group headed by Robert Millar in Elohim City, Oklahoma."

Following the Oklahoma City bombing, the militia movement came under intense government scrutiny. The media revealed that both suspects, Timothy McVeigh and Terry Nichols, had attended militia meetings in Michigan. Federal prosecutors charged that McVeigh's motivation in the bombing was his intense hatred of the federal government for its destruction of the Branch Davidian complex. Moreover, media reports claimed that McVeigh's favorite book was the notorious *Turner Diaries*, written by former American Nazi Party leader William Pierce, the founder of the National Alliance. The *Diaries*, billed by the neo-Nazi National Alliance as a "handbook for white victory," is a primer for race war masquerading as a violent fantasy novel.

Written in 1978, *The Turner Diaries* proved an inspiration to the Order. "Today has been the day of the rope—a grim and bloody day but an unavoidable one.... But the night is filled with silent horrors from tens of thousands of lampposts, power poles and trees throughout this vast metropolitan area, the grisly forms hang.... There are many thousands of hanging female corpses like that in the city tonight, all wearing identical placards around their necks. They are the white women who are married to or living with blacks, with Jews, or with other non-white males," Pierce wrote.

Pierce, like Thomas, lives in a state bordering Ohio, near the community of Millpoint, West Virginia. The Church of the Creator (COTC), one of the most vicious American racist organizations, sold its property in North Carolina to Pierce in September 1992. The COTC operated openly on High Street in the Ohio State campus area during the late '80s and early 1990s. Under the leadership of Joey Hagar, neo-Nazi skinheads terrorized the campus community culminating in the murder of a black woman. Their cry was "RAHOWA!" (RAcial HOly WAr). That incident, and intense pressure of anti-racist activists caused the demise of the local organization.

The climate for racist recruiting is ripe. As Floyd Cochran likes to point out, David Duke's 1990 political agenda is now virtually mainstream Republicanism: destroy affirmative action because it's taking white guys' jobs away, keep those dirty spics out of California, kick those promiscuous black welfare mothers off public assistance, stop Big Government regulations, build more prisons, and gut education. In the economic transition from an urban-industrial to a high-tech, post-industrial suburban society, lawmakers decided to use ordinary people as the shock absorbers on the rough ride to the 21st century.

To many at the bottom, trickle-down looks like trickle-on

economics. An industrial state like Ohio is an easy place to find displaced factory workers and small farmers desperately wanting someone to blame for their problems. These disgruntled white men are more than willing to listen to Rush Limbaugh or even the Klan, who basically offer the same scapegoats: blacks, gays, Big Government conspiracies, liberals, feminists and immigrants.

A 1995 *Klanwatch Intelligence Report* listed the following hate groups as active in Ohio: the International Ku Klux Klan in Sandusky, Knight Riders in Ross, Knights of the KKK in Columbus, Northern Knights and Aryan Nations in Dayton, Aryan Racial Loyalist Party and White Christian Guard in Euclid, National Alliance in Parma, the G.A. Kleve Propaganda Ministry in Maple Heights.

The racist targeting of Ohio has spawned a homegrown anti-racist response. Anti-Racist Action (ARA), perhaps the fastest growing anti-racist organization in the nation, is headquartered in the north campus area in Columbus. ARA spokesperson and co-founder Jim McNamara has long argued that government officials are making a big mistake by pushing the "just ignore them" line. Ex-Aryan Nations official Cochran agrees, advising ARA members to protest their presence so it's harder for them to recruit.

"It's true that the number of real, live American Nazis is small right now, but don't tell us to just ignore them. Don't tell us they're just a joke," said McNamara. "Tell it to the friends of Eric Freeman, the 11-year-old white kid killed by his older brothers David and Brian, under the inspiration of Mark Thomas. Tell it to the families who lost loved ones in the Oklahoma City bombing. Tell it to the cops that were just shot at by the Kehoe brothers. I hate to say 'we told you so,' but they're not a joke. They're for real and they kill."

The Detroit-based Resistance Records is part of the racist movement using rock music with a hate message to recruit young people. A Resistance Records music festival in Cleveland in 1995 drew some 500 racist "boneheads." ARA, comprised mostly of college students, makes it a point to bring its message of racial harmony to challenge the hate spewed at the racist concerts.

An alliance of ARA activists, Barry Edney's Ordinary People's Movement and Cornell McCleary's Coalition of Concerned Black Citizens, in conjunction with the local NAACP, may have come up with the best tactic to combat racists. Their 'outing' of Klan members in 1995, by taking busloads of people to the homes of known white supremacists, appears to have shaken the racists up in Ohio. This action, despite being widely denounced by Columbus' power structure and the mainstream media, made a lasting impact on Klan leader Tony Gamble.

Under oath, Gamble said, "There's seven Ron Lee's" in his KKK organization: "These people don't want their name to be shown on TV because if anti-protesters found out where they lived, they would bring busloads of people and picket up and down in front of their nice homes. They have good jobs. They don't want to lose their jobs."

Ignore them, politicians say, and they'll go away. In reality, they'll go to the churches, the high schools, the campuses and preach their doctrine of hate and the toxic Nazi slime will continue to ooze in from Idaho, Washington, Pennsylvania, Michigan, West Virginia and elsewhere.

March 5, 1997

Those Crazy Kehoes

Those cagey Kehoe brothers, Cheyne and Chevie, are at it again. A *Columbus Dispatch* news headline had the boys insisting they weren't "white supremacists." The *Dispatch* pretty much took this at face value. What else is new?

The Kehoe brothers are awaiting trial following their February 1997 shoot-out with Ohio state troopers in Wilmington. A nationwide manhunt ended on June 16, 1997, when Cheyne turned himself in and squealed that his brother was hiding at a Utah farm. Cheyne faces numerous criminal charges including a 16-count indictment in Ohio stemming from the shoot-out. I suspect his anticipation of sharing the next few years in close quarters with a prison population that is disproportionately black, due to our racist justice system, has Cheyne denying his faith.

Cheyne can run, but he cannot hide from the statement he read when he turned himself in, that clearly confirms his allegiance to white supremacy. "The reason I acted in the manner I did was due to the actions of men like Randy Weaver, Gordon Kahl and Bob Matthews.... The government and law enforcement agencies abused the individual rights of these men," Cheyne stated.

Let's examine his unholy trinity one by one.

Weaver, a virulent anti-Semite, believes that the U.S. government is under the control of an international Jewish conspiracy. He frequently visited the Hayden Lake, Idaho, compound of the Aryan Nations. There he could discuss his racist conspiracy theories that ZOG—the Zionist Occupational Government—runs the United States.

Weaver became a far-right icon after he was injured and wife and son were killed in a shoot-out with federal agents in August 1992 at Ruby Ridge, Idaho. During the siege, neo-Nazi "boneheads" and Aryan Nations members rallied to support Weaver. Aryan Nations Ambassador at Large Louis Beam co-founded a Weaver support group, Citizens United for Justice.

In 1994, under the slogan, "No More Wacos, No More Weavers," the militia movement exploded nationwide. Its organizational roots are linked to 150 ultra-right-wing leaders who met in Estes Park, Colorado, on October 23, 1992, and gave birth to the militia strategy. The event was hosted by Christian Identity Pastor Pete Peters, a white supremacist theologian and hate-monger.

The Kehoes claim Christian Identity as their religion. The religion preaches that Jews are the spawn of Satan and black are "mudpeople" without souls.

No racists here, Cheyne?

In 1983, Gordon Kahl was an active member of the Posse Comitatus, a loosely organized band of Christian Identity anti-government activists. Kahl murdered two federal marshals in North Dakota, and like the Kehoe brothers, became a fugitive. Rather than surrender, Kahl died in a shoot-out with Arkansas law enforcement officers where a local sheriff was also killed. Kahl is considered a martyr by the Posse Comitatus, Aryan Nations and other white supremacists like the Kehoes.

Finally, we come to Matthews, perhaps America's slimiest pond scum. Matthews founded The Order in 1983, a terrorist organization that robbed banks and armored trucks to fund neo-Nazi activities. The Order murdered Jewish talk radio host Alan Berg in June '94. Matthews died in December of that year after a 36-hour fire-fight with law enforcement officers.

I suppose Cheyne's heroes weren't "white supremacists" either, just misunderstood.

August 13, 1997

He Ain't Chevie,
He's My Brother

With Tim McVeigh convicted and sentenced to death and Terry Nichols imprisoned for life for the April 19, 1995, Oklahoma City bombing, John Doe Number Two and "others unknown" remain on the loose. And the best place to look is in the white supremacist, terrorist underground.

Cheyne Keyhoe's recent confession that "I do have knowledge of my brother's involvement in the bombing of a federal building" must be taken seriously. The FBI's immediate announcement that it would probe any connections between McVeigh and Chevie Keyhoe is long overdue. Chevie, an admitted white supremacist, had ties to both the Aryan Nations in the Idaho panhandle and the white supremacist compound in Elohim City, Oklahoma.

Telephone records prove that McVeigh called the Elohim compound on April 5, 1995, just two weeks before the bombing. Also, on October 12, 1993, McVeigh was ticketed within 10 miles of Elohim City on County Route 220, the only access road into the racist compound. Was McVeigh looking for a place to hide after the blast?

McVeigh's highly publicized motive of avenging the Waco massacre eclipses the equally important significance of the

April 19, 1995, date for white supremacists. A few hours after McVeigh and John Doe Number Two lit the fuse to the Ryder fertilizer and fuel truck bomb, racist cop-killer Richard Snell was executed in an Arkansas prison. His body was brought to Elohim City by the Reverend Robert Millar for a white supremacist "martyr funeral."

It's also well established that McVeigh took his cues from the neo-Nazi novel, *The Turner Diaries* by William Pierce, a primer for inciting racial civil war in America. Anti-racist activists and investigators have long been fascinated with the testimony of a former manager of the Shadows Motel outside of Spokane, Washington. The manager told authorities that "Days before the bombing, he [Chevie Keyhoe] mentioned to me that there's going to be something happening on the 19th and it's going to wake people up." The manager described Chevie as "ecstatic" when a news flash reported the terrorists' bombing.

Chevie, currently facing trial in our state for a shoot-out with state troopers near the Aryan Nations headquarters in New Vienna, Ohio, was also indicted in December in Arkansas on seven counts of murder, racketeering and conspiracy to bring about an "all-white, Aryan People's Republic." Prosecutors claim that Chevie planned to create their racist republic through "a campaign of murder, robberies and kidnappings," according to the Associated Press.

As part of that indictment, Chevie was specifically charged with "transporting stolen goods from the white supremacist community of Elohim City, Oklahoma, to Spokane in March 1995"—a month before the bombing.

Additionally, Chevie is charged with directing his Aryan Republic cohorts to murder gun dealer William Mueller, his wife Nancy and Nancy's eight-year-old daughter in 1996.

Chevie, prosecutors claim, became fascinated with Robert Matthews and his neo-Nazi terrorist organization, The Order.

Following the conviction of Terry Nichols, the jury fore-woman Niki Deutchman said, "I think a decision was made early on that McVeigh and Nichols were the ones they were looking for. The same resources were not used to try and find out who else might be responsible." The trial also made it clear that Nichols was not the individual seen with Tim McVeigh just prior to the explosions. Stephen Jones, McVeigh's trial attorney, is writing a book examining the involvement of other racist suspects in the bombing. You can bet Chevie's name will be in the book.

Jones reportedly will elaborate on evidence that he was not allowed to introduce at McVeigh's trial. The evidence suggests that the Oklahoma bombing was planned at Elohim City. An Oklahoma grand jury is already investigating these issues.

Cheyne's recent trial revelation that "Chevie asked me to get involved in the Aryan People's Republic, a white supremacist movement" is anything but shocking. Arkansas' *Democrat Gazette* noted that Chevie's criminal charges stemmed from his desire "to foment a revolution by the creation of a white power group, The Aryan People's Republic."

Clinton County, Ohio, Assistant Prosecutor Rick Moyer's January 1998 comments to the *Columbus Dispatch* are well worth remembering: "The white supremacist issue is for some other trial in some other time and place...all I am trying is a man who came into Wilmington and fired at two law-enforce-ment officers."

A bizarre and curious comment from a county prosecutor. The Keyhoe brothers shoot-out with state troopers coincided with Aryan Nations' first public rally at the Ohio Statehouse. What were the Keyhoes doing in Ohio? Did they visit the New

Vienna complex? What does Cheyne know about Chevie's involvement in the bombing of a federal building?

February 4, 1998

Springtime For Hitler

Neo-Nazi propaganda is sprouting in the campus area. Anti-Racist Action activists report finding National Alliance fliers from as far north as 18th Avenue to as far south as West Eighth Avenue. The fliers would make Goebbels proud.

Perhaps you've seen them—the text on the fliers is identical, but it comes with two different pictures. One has a young Aryan poster child doing her homework in a seemingly blissful suburban setting; the other has a preschooler with a puppy on the lawn. The headline blares: "She Needs The Truth" and asks "Where Will She Find It?"

Not, according to the National Alliance, "On television, with its racially mixed couples and multicultural propaganda" or "In her classroom, which has been converted into a neo-Communist brainwashing pen" or "On the streets, where she stands a greater than one in four chance of being raped, probably by a non-white."

The National Alliance assures the reader: "We are here to make sure that more and more young people like her will have access."

I don't claim to have "truth" like the National Alliance, but I do know some facts about them. The organization, National Youth Alliance, sprang from the hate-filled 1968 George Wallace for President campaign. Its goal: "To liquidate the enemies of the American people." Initially controlled by Willis Carto, the head honcho behind the anti-Semitic Liberty Lobby, the group became ardent admirers of Adolf Hitler. They sell and promote Francis Parker Yockey's *Imperium*, a 600-page tome intended as the "second Mein Kampf."

In 1970, former members of George Lincoln Rockwell's American Nazi Party split with Carto and renamed the organization the National Alliance. It's fearless leader: William L. Pierce, an American Nazi and author of the infamous *Turner Diaries*. Convicted Oklahoma City bomber Timothy McVeigh was an avid reader and enthusiastic proselytizer of the *Turner Diaries*, a primer for promoting race war in America. There is a graphic and strikingly similar account between the bombing of the Murrah Federal Building in Oklahoma City and a bombing in the *Diaries*.

Pierce professes that his calling in life is to "save white people from themselves." He runs his neo-Nazi organization from a isolated, heavily wooded 400-acre compound in West Virginia. Recently, National Alliance members were indicted in Florida as part of an alleged 12-state terror network with plans to plant bombs around Disneyland to distract the police so they could rob banks for their movement.

The most disturbing thing about the flier is the local post office box in Hilliard, Ohio, given as the address. These neo-Nazis stand for death and genocide. If you know who they are, out them.

May 28, 1998

OSU History X

White supremacists and neo-Nazis continue to be supported by local so-called conservatives with ties to the Republican Party. The latest, and one of the most flagrant recent examples, is Ohio State University student Matt Ball's guest column in the *Observer*, a right-wing newspaper that's distributed for free in the campus area.

The *Observer* describes itself as "an independently run student newspaper published by the Buckeye Conservative Studies Foundation." In fact, it's a noticeably low-rent cousin to the notorious *Dartmouth Review*, which won its 15 minutes of fame when its staffers attempted to dismantle the anti-apartheid shantytown erected by students at the Ivy League school to protest South Africa's white supremacist policies in the 1980s.

In the past few years, an inexcusable—and often ignored by the mainstream media—pattern of behavior has emerged wherein so-called conservative Republicans give aid and comfort to explicit racists and anti-Semites. Recall that after the 1992 election, investigative reporter Russ Bellant linked then-Ohio Governor George Voinovich to money sources provided by Eastern and Central European former Nazis and fascists.

Columbus Alive reported that the Republican Ohio House Speaker Pro Tem William G. Batchelder , was listed as a member of the little-known and highly secretive far-right Council for National Policy.

More recently, we had President Bill Clinton's chief accuser in the House, Representative Robert Barr, and Senator Trent Lott contributing columns to a white supremacist organization, the Council of Conservative Citizens.

Which brings us back to the *Observer* and Matt Ball. Above an ad for the College Republicans, a typical *Observer* article offers the lead, "Newt!, Newt!, Newt!, the crowd of young and old roared," under the headline "Newt Speaks at Notre Dame."

But the real politics of the editors are revealed by their choice of guest columnists. First, Andy Rufus ponders, if the recently tortured and slain Matthew Shepard "was not gay and had merely been robbed, would we have heard about it?" and wonders, "How long will it be until being a Clinton hater is a federal offense?"

While Rufus is merely sophomoric, Ball's *Observer* column is sinister. After pointing out that there are "17 organizations I found for black/African students" and "nine organizations I found for Jewish students," Ball uses the *Observer* as a recruiting tool to form a "European-American" student organization at OSU. This is an old tactic, a la David Duke and his infamous National Association for the Advancement of White People. The *Observer* staff are either ignoramuses, dupes or willing pawns of neo-Nazi organizing techniques. Sure, the *Observer* editors will try to falsely hide behind free speech claims, but remember the axiom, only the government can censor. The *Observer* editors made a constitutionally protected editorial decision to publish these racist sentiments.

Ball is a frequent writer of letters to the editor to the Ohio State student paper, the *Lantern*. In a May 22, 1998, letter to the *Lantern*, Ball proudly admitted to putting up National Alliance fliers in the campus area. The fliers contained Aryan-type poster children with warnings against "Jewish-controlled

Hollywood," and stated that the blue-eyed, blonde lass pictured "stands a greater than one in four chance in being raped, probably by a non-white."

A week later, Ball wrote that "there is ample evidence to show that Jewish losses during World War II are nowhere close to 6 million." And, he pointed out, "CNN is no longer owned by a Gentile, neither is CBS, ABC, nor Disney. Don't let me forget Time Warner, the *New York Times*, the *Wall Street Journal* and the *U.S. News and World Report*. All are controlled by Jews."

Ball is so proud of his National Alliance membership that he's featured on the neo-Nazi group's web page. It would have only taken *Observer* editors a few minutes to research the National Alliance.

Anti-Racist Action activists are busy posting fliers exposing Ball's neo-Nazi connections. But who in the Republican Party or the conservative movement will dare demand that their comrades at the *Observer* be held accountable for serving as a propaganda tool for an organization dedicated to genocidal terror?

June 10, 1999

Portrait Of A Racist

The neo-Nazi apologists and propagandists are busy feeding the public misinformation and distancing themselves from their boy, Benjamin Smith—the racist serial killer who went on a shooting spree over the weekend of July 4, 1999. They're blaming the Bloomington, Indiana, police who ticketed Smith for littering after his racist hate sheets flew off cars.

Smith was a member of the World Church of the Creator, a neo-Nazi terrorist organization. He went on his rampage only hours after the church's anointed "Pontifex Maximus," the "Reverend" Matt Hale, lost his appeal to get a license to practice law in Illinois because of his racist beliefs and total disdain for the U.S. government and its laws. It's hard to swear an oath as an "Officer of the Court" when you apparently want to destroy it.

Hale's "church," based in East Peoria, Illinois, has a long documented history of racist violence. It's also one of the fastest growing racist organizations in the U.S.—going from eight churches in early 1995 to 31 today. Church of the Creator "Reverend" George Loeb murdered African-American Harold Mansfield Jr. on May 17, 1991, in Florida. "Reverend" Joey Hagar was convicted after killing an African-American woman in Columbus during that same time period. Shortly after Smith's bloody spree, police seized white supremacist literature from the home of the Williams brothers, Benjamin Matthew and James Tyler, suspects in the murder of a gay couple in northern California and arson attacks on three Sacramento synagogues. The Associated Press reported that police investigators are "examining whether the case is part of a wide hate-crime conspiracy and whether the brothers are linked to the World Church of the Creator."

Who's responsible for Smith's actions? The "liberal" media? What liberal media? You mean the mainstream corporate media that sucks up and spits out every lie and distortion "Reverend" Hale has to offer? Remember how the media dutifully noted Hale's absurd disclaimer that his organization does not practice or advocate violence?

Let's look to the words of the church founder, Ben Klassen, in his 1987 tome *RAHOWA! The Planet is All Ours*. Klassen told his "congregation" that they should prepare for "RAHOWA! [Racial Holy War]: In the one word we sum up the total goal and program of not only the Church of the Creator, but of the total white race... We regard it as a holy war to the finish—a racial holy war. RAHOWA! is inevitable. It is the ultimate and only solution... No longer can the mud races and the white race live on the same planet and survive."

Remember also that the mainstream media bought Hale's big lie when he said that Smith quit the church in May 1999. The small non-profit Center for New Community almost instantly issued a special report on Smith, overlooked by the for-profit corporate media, pointing out that the Church of the Creator's June 1999 newsletter announced that Smith "has relocated to central Illinois to assist PM Hale at World Headquarters." If he quit, why was he moving to the East Peoria headquarters?

Obviously, the school year was over at Indiana University in

Bloomington and the church's "Creator of the Year" was heeding the head racist's national call to move to Illinois.

The center's special report on Smith notes that a July 1998 directive from Hale to Church of the Creator members announced: "Just as Adolph Hitler knew that before he could win Germany, he must first win his home turf, Munich and then Bavaria as a whole, before we can win the world, I fervently believe that we must win our capital, Illinois... Therefore, I am calling on all of you (particularly my most dedicated brothers and sisters) to strongly consider moving to Illinois, central Illinois in particular... We will get the ball rolling. RAHOWA!"

Liberal media, my ass. Unless ignoring the obvious and buying racist terrorist spin is a new definition of "liberal."

Following the words of their fuehrer, New Jersey neo-Nazi organization Day of the Rope Productions joined Hale and his pals in Illinois. The Ropesters take their name from the fictional day, described as "necessary and bloody," in the neo-Nazi novel *The Turner Diaries*. This is the day when all white "race traitors," Jews and people of color are publicly hung from lamp posts.

Tim McVeigh loved the book and recommended it highly, and the Klan members in Texas who put a rope around James Byrd and dragged him till there were few parts of his body left said they were "starting *The Turner Diaries* tonight," according to sworn statements.

The author of *The Turner Diaries*, William Pierce, is an avowed neo-Nazi. He also wrote another fictional primer to promote racial holy war titled *Hunter*. In it, a "lone wolf" racial terrorist rampages through the streets shooting "race traitors" at random, and targets an interracial couple.

Who's responsible for Smith's actions? The liberals who

preach tolerance and diversity or the neo-Nazi terrorist network that pumps out propaganda by the tons, harasses, targets and kills non-whites, burns synagogues and preaches genocide as the final solution?

July 15, 1999

White Man's Bible

Exactly what part of "neo-Nazi terrorist network" doesn't the mainstream media and middle-class America understand? In the aftermath of Buford Furrow's August 1999 shooting spree—which wounded five Jewish people, including four kids, and killed a Filipino-American—isn't the simple-minded slogan "Ignore them, they'll just go away" fully discredited? Nobody can ignore the growing violent white supremacist and neo-Nazi movement.

Can it happen in Columbus? It already has. From 1989 to 1991, between 20 to 30 campus-based racist skinheads, or "boneheads," openly operated in Columbus. The boneheads were members of the Church of the Creator.

Just a month before Furrow's bloody spree, Benjamin Smith of the offshoot group World Church of the Creator went on a rampage that targeted Jews, African-Americans and Asian-Americans, killing two. Smith's progenitors of neo-Nazi ideology in Columbus were local Creator leaders John Reid and Matthew Hayhow. John Backstrom, a local music promoter, was violently assaulted by Reid and nine other neo-Nazis in April 1990. Backstrom informed the police that he recognized all 10 of his bonehead assailants, yet assault charges were only brought against Reid. Hayhow and Reid were sentenced in March 1993 with a third man for robbing two Columbus banks in 1990.

With the "Reverend" Hayhow in prison, Joey Hager took control as the Creator's "holy man" in Columbus. In August 1992, Hager stabbed 19-year-old African-American Nichele Trice to death in an altercation on 18th Avenue; in February 1993, Hager was sentenced to eight to 25 years in prison for voluntary manslaughter. Oddly, Hager's judge deemed his well-known involvement with the neo-Nazi Creators to be irrelevant and inadmissible at the trial. After the trial, *Columbus Alive* rather easily examined Hager's personal papers and effects, including his personal copy of *The White Man's Bible*, which lays out the five basic racist beliefs of the Creators: our race is our religion; the white race is nature's finest; racial loyalty is the greatest honor; racial treason is the worst crime; and what is good for the white race is good for nature.

The daily *Columbus Dispatch* ignored or downplayed Hager's neo-Nazi connections. Only the nonprofit journal *Columbus Free Press* and the now-defunct weekly *Columbus Guardian*, which pointed out that Trice's killing was not even counted as a hate crime, covered the racist nature of the murder.

In March 1993, another local man with neo-Nazi ties, John W. Gerhardt, was sentenced to three to 10 years for abduction. Gerhardt sought sanctuary at the Aryan Nations' compound in Hayden Lake, Idaho, after attempting to kidnap a woman from a Bank One ATM machine in a central Ohio suburb. He hid out with the Aryans in 1991 until his arrest in May 1992.

Gerhardt and his brother Edward both attended Columbus' Mifflin High School and first attracted national attention when they founded the American White Nationalist Party in 1972, according to the *Guardian*. Gerhardt currently is serving time in the Orient Correctional Facility, where prison sources say he's an Aryan Nations minister. Prison sources also report that he recently converted former Ohio Grand Titan of the Knights of the Ku Klux Klan Vince Pinette away from the Klan to the neo-Nazi movement. Just a couple of white guys, doing time and talking hate.

Columbus plays a prominent role in the neo-Nazi movement, particularly in relationship to bank robbers. Aryan Nations offshoot the Order, led by Robert J. Matthews, stole $4 million and killed Jewish talk show host Alan Berg in 1984. Matthews died in a shoot-out with FBI agents in 1984, but not before he visited Columbus. In the book *The Silent Brotherhood*, the rise and fall of the Order is depicted, including Matthews' Columbus excursion "where he met a college history professor he knew through the National Alliance." The authors fail to name the professor, whose identity was redacted from government documents.

Between January 1994 and January 1996, Aryan Republican Army Commander Peter Kevin Langan committed as many as 22 bank robberies before his arrest at a south-side Columbus safe house, according to FBI testimony. In 1995, Langan recorded a two-hour recruitment video for his Aryan army, where he displayed a copy of Richard Hoskin's book *Vigilante Christendom*. He called it a "handbook for revolution."

Police also found a Hoskin book in Furrow's abandoned van. Hoskin, a racist Christian Identity preacher, advocates a "Phineas Priesthood" of underground racist terrorist "kamikazes" or "Shiite warriors" who kill non-whites and race-mixers. Hoskin draws from the Bible (Book of Numbers, 25:1-18) to defend the killing of interracial couples.

When Aryan Nations staged a rally in Columbus in February 1997, a member of the racist Southside Greathouse armed robbery gang—the gang that went on a 19-day crime spree in October 1997—shot and critically wounded a black newspaper carrier. An FBI agent told Judge James Graham that the shooting was both random and racially motivated. Furrow's shooting spree resembles those outlined in National Alliance founder William Pierce's novels *The Turner Diaries* and *Hunter.* Both glorify terrorism and random assassination of non-Aryan people.

San Diego-based Alex Curtis, who also has neo-Nazi ties, praised Furrow for his "lone wolf" tactics. "[Jews] deserve the retribution that lone wolves are just beginning to dish out. Now a major sacrifice of Jews and niggers occurs once a month or so. Imagine the near future when the number rises to once a week," Curtis wrote in his weekly e-mail magazine. "We are witnessing the end of civil society. A race-mixing society that must die if our race is to survive."

Exposing these beliefs is our first line of defense against future bloodshed, if we want to stop the next Benjamin Smith or Buford Furrow before their hatred becomes deadly.

August 19, 1999

Nazis In The Heartland

Will Ohio be the nation's heartland for neo-Nazi terror? The WCMH-TV news report on the National Alliance's leafleting in the Dublin and Grove City areas will come as no surprise to regular readers of this column. Erich Gliebe, of Cleveland, told Channel 4 that the organization targeted the two Columbus suburbs because the areas were "most receptive to their messages," according to producer Karen Baker.

The alliance is a West Virginia-based neo-Nazi organization headed for two decades by William Pierce. In the past few years, National Alliance membership has grown dramatically, operating in more than a dozen states.

Pierce calls Gliebe, a former amateur boxer, a "tireless recruiter and organizer, a man who has spent nearly every available minute working for the alliance." Gliebe's Cleveland organization is the single largest in the alliance, boasting some 60 open neo-Nazis and hosting an annual "Euro-American Cultural Fest." A recent intelligence report from the Southern Poverty Law Center (SPLC), an organization that monitors white supremacist groups, named Gliebe one of the elite "dirty dozen" of white supremacist leaders in the U.S.

Gliebe serves as the National Alliance's Midwest spokesperson and regional coordinator. His cultural fest has drawn the likes of Pierce, Tom Metzger, head of the neo-Nazi White

Aryan Resistance, and Steve Barry, editor of the white supremacist magazine *The Resister*. Not far behind in the alliance hier-
archy is Hilliard's Matt Ball, also seen on Channel 4's January
16, 2000, report.

The influence of the Idaho-based Aryan Nations is begin-
ning to fade as the health of its founder, the ailing and aged
Richard Butler, 81, declines. Meanwhile, Pierce and the
National Alliance appear to be growing stronger by the day.
The alliance is busy building bridges to other fascist and white
supremacist groups. Just last summer, the SPLC reported that
Pierce and two "gussied-up skinheads" dined at the exclusive
Washington, D.C., University Club with former Reagan
Whitehouse staffer and GOP strategist Todd Blodgett.

Blodgett, a protégé of the late Lee Atwater, a key GOP campaign strategist for both Presidents Reagan and Bush, is the
son of wealthy Republican State Representative Gary Blodgett
of Iowa. On April 26, 1999, Pierce and Blodgett incorporated
Resistance Records LLC in the District of Columbia, according
to the SPLC. The deal gave the National Alliance control over
a defunct racist record company.

In October last year, Pierce went public with the fact that he
now owned Resistance Records, the largest catalog and inventory of "white power" music in the U.S. A few years ago, prior
to its demise, the record company was selling an estimated
50,000 white supremacist CDs every year.

The alliance's strategy is to reach out to both young neo-
Nazi shock troops and older, more mainstream racist organiza-
tions with Republican ties, like the Council of Conservative
Citizens (CCC). Two recent reports from the SPLC—*Money,
Music and the Doctor* and *Sharks in the Mainstream*—document
Pierce's activities. The CCC is little more than the reincarna-
tion of the racist White Citizen's Councils of the '50s and '60s.

In 1999, during the Clinton impeachment trials, news reports documented that Senate Majority Leader Trent Lott, a Republican from Mississippi, and Representative Bob Barr, a Republican from Georgia, both wrote for the CCC's racist newsletter.

The CCC and the National Alliance have many things in common, including attacking the Martin Luther King Jr. holiday, Black History Month and affirmative action. The CCC refuses to disclose the names of its members, but the SPLC collected the names of 175 CCC members and "found a significant number of members have been linked to unabashedly racist groups including the Invisible Empire, Knights of the Ku Klux Klan, the Carolina Knights of the Ku Klux Klan, the National Association for the Advancement of White People, the America First Party and the neo-Nazi National Alliance."

The CCC's leader, Gordon Lee Baum, attempted to recruit Vince Reed, the head of security for the Aryan Nations, to the CCC's national board in 1995, according to Reed. The council has also been endorsed by Senator Jesse Helms, a Republican from North Carolina, and various Republican politicians, particularly in the South. Council leaders have claimed responsibility for the defeat of former South Carolina Governor David Beasley, who angered the group by opposing the continued flying of the Confederate battle flag over the state's capital building.

It makes perfect sense that the National Alliance would pass out information attacking the Martin Luther King holiday the day before the event, and less than two months before the Ohio primary. The emergence of a highly emotional and polarizing political "wedge" issue, as Atwater liked to call them, comes at an opportune time for George W. Bush's presidential campaign in Ohio. Recall his father was elected as an anti-civil rights "states' rights" representative from Texas in 1966, and his son is now busy defending the states' rights of South Carolina to fly the Confederate flag. Pierce and his central Ohio and Cleveland lackeys may simply be priming the pump for Bush.

January 20, 2000

Ohio: Home Of Hate

Will the neo-Nazi Aryan Nations organization relocate its headquarters to Ohio? Floyd Cochran, former director of propaganda for the hate group, now a leading anti-racist activist, concedes that there's been "a lot of speculation" on a move by the group from their Hayden Lake, Idaho, compound to southwest Ohio.

Why the Buckeye State? There's the failing health of 80-year-old Richard Butler, the founder and leader of both the Aryan Nations and the Church of Jesus Christ Christian. Butler is the United States' most infamous Christian Identity preacher—a neo-Nazi ideology masquerading as religion that preaches Anglo-Saxons and Aryans are God's "only" chosen people. News reports say Butler has willed his 20-acre Idaho home and complex to his daughters, who've distanced themselves from his beliefs.

A year ago, the Southern Poverty Law Center sued Butler personally, his church, Aryan Nations and Saphire Inc., an Idaho corporation, in hopes of seizing the neo-Nazi organization's assets in a civil suit. The suit claims, "Members of the [Aryan Nations] security force chased them [Victoria and Jason Keenan] for over two miles, shot at them with assault rifles, detained them, battered them, and threatened to kill them." The center, successful in the past in suing white supremacist groups and seizing their assets, could force the Aryans to search for a new home.

Cochran describes the Hayden Lake compound as the "crown jewel" of the Aryan movement. "Take it away and there is no Aryan Nations," he told *Columbus Alive*. He says a likely place for the homeless neo-Nazis to head is New Vienna, Ohio. Harold Ray "Butch" Redfeairn, Butler's personal aide and most likely successor, set up a regional Midwest Aryan Nations center there in 1997.

Cochran points out that the Midwest is potentially much more fertile recruiting ground for white supremacist hate organizations than Butler's Northwest network. White supremacist David Duke, a former Nazi and Klan leader, understood this when he made southern Ohio part of an all-white homeland (to be founded after the United States is shattered).

"Most of the white supremacists seek out mountains and hills in their belief that this is where God's chosen people should flee in preparation for the final days," Cochran explained. "Draw a line from the Alleghenies in Pennsylvania down through Appalachia in its foothills and you're going to pick up a lot of white Anglo-Saxon Protestant and white supremacist organizations."

A brief comparison of hate groups available to an Ohio-centered Aryan Nations versus an Idaho-based neo-Nazi movement yields disturbing numbers. Idaho has nine hate groups compared to Ohio's 22—the seventh largest total in the U.S. The state of Wyoming, Idaho's neighbor, has one hate group; the Columbus suburb of Hilliard alone has two hate groups.

This concentration of hate is seen throughout the Midwest, but not the West, according to the latest Southern Poverty Law Center data. Pennsylvania has 27 hate groups. Montana has five; Michigan 24. Oregon 10 versus Indiana's 17. Washington and Illinois are a wash at 17 each. Heading south, 10 hate groups call Kentucky home, compared to Nevada's two. Let's see, that makes it 117 hate groups in the Midwest to 44 in the West—a rout in favor of Ohio being the country's heart of it all for hatred.

Of course, it may be difficult to continue the Idaho Aryan Nations' hate legacy in Ohio. Butler's organization spawned our country's foremost domestic terrorist group, The Order, in the 1980s and just last August one of Butler's former security men, Buford O. Furrow Jr., was charged with attacking a Jewish community center in Los Angeles and killing a non-white mailman. Three months later, Butler's Denver organizer, Nathan Thill, confessed on television that he murdered a black man because he was "wearing the enemy's uniform"—his black skin.

Still, Redfeairn managed in a short period of time to sow violence from his base in western Clinton County, Ohio. Last July, Kale T. Kelly, Redfeairn's New Vienna lieutenant, was convicted on weapons charges stemming from an alleged plot to gather an arsenal to attack the government. In February 1997, the Kehoe brothers with ties to the Aryan Nations shot it out with Clinton County sheriff's deputies and Ohio State troopers before fleeing the state. Most analysts suggest the brothers were heading up to Columbus for the Aryan Nations' Statehouse rally, which drew scores of other white supremacist groups. Remember that the leader of the Aryan Republican Army, aka the Midwest Bank Bandits, was captured in Columbus after the neo-Nazi group carried out 22 bank robberies in the mid-1990s in order to fund a white supremacist revolution.

The nation's fastest growing neo-Nazi group, the National Alliance, is already well-entrenched here with the organization's strongest chapter in Cleveland and a burgeoning central Ohio organization.

February 3, 2000

Nazis In Newark

The day after Adolf Hitler's birthday, April 21, 2001, the November 9th Society plans to march through Newark and hold a rally at Everett Park. The organization draws its name from Kristallnacht, the "Night of Broken Glass," when Hitler's Nazi thugs attacked Jewish-owned businesses throughout Germany, breaking windows and terrorizing Jewish families.

These neo-Nazi stormtroopers are on an organizing and recruiting campaign with a clear agenda—to target and attack blacks, Jews and anyone to the left of Mussolini. Their slogan is simple: "Taking National Socialism into the 21st Century." Their elaborate website goes into great detail on how to "organize a resistance movement," and the society's ties to Hitler are clear: "Like the heroes and heroines of the Third Reich, you may choose to answer the call to *idealism and sacrifice.*"

Here's their advice for getting involved: "If you love your country but fear your government, becoming an underground activist may give you the mechanism you need to start making a difference."

"Freedom is sustained by three boxes—the ballot box, the jury box and the ammo box. Unfortunately, more and more concerned citizens are becoming increasingly alarmed by what they see as the dangerously weakened condition of the ballot box and the jury box," the November 9th Society argues.

The organization offers "information" from "official counter-insurgency training manuals" in order to bring about the Fourth Reich in the United States. The neo-Nazi society's website includes step-by-step instructions for creating a terrorist underground organization. Of course they run a disclaimer, after providing the information, noting that the "November 9th Society does not endorse, condone, or encourage any illegal act," and the how-to manuals for fostering race war in the United States are "presented for information, research, entertainment and educational purposes only."

The November 9th Society is part of a growing, global neo-Nazi network and boasts ties with British, German, Irish, Scottish and Romanian counterparts that are organizing terrorism in hopes of ushering in a Fourth Reich and a Third World War. I'm not kidding. Take a look at their own words: "Only Adolf Hitler and his devoted legions stood against the whole world in order to destroy the culture-destroying Marxist communism, and brought about a cultural renaissance the likes that have never been seen before nor since."

Despite their bad grammar, their message can't be mistaken: "He [Hitler] may have lost the war, but the battle has just begun, and any straight-minded white person can just look around and see that he was right."

"His [Hitler's] book *Mein Kampf* has only been outsold by the Holy Bible and is a political testament and partial autobiography. It has been described as a 'beacon of light in a stormy sea of doubt,'" the society's website offers.

As I've written in the past, it's my belief that white supremacists and neo-Nazis are targeting the state of Ohio with the goal of fostering a race war. They're here to recruit members and form separatist armed compounds leading directly to guerrilla warfare.

But you needn't trust my opinions, since the November 9th Society spells out "Step 3" on its website as: "BEGIN GUERRILLA OPERATIONS."

"A resistance movement will often need to use *counterterror* to intimidate traitors, collaborators and informers," the society claims. As a known race traitor—that is, somebody who believes in universal human rights for all people—I plan to cover the rally and report on these terrorists. The best way to deal with Nazi terrorists is to confront them directly and not wait for their numbers to grow.

Their agenda is defined in their own words. They are urging their membership to move from "passive resistance, [to] active resistance, [to] guerrilla warfare, [to] open insurrection, and civil war."

For right-wing fans of school vouchers and government support for faith-based schools, the neo-Nazis boast that they've already got in place "a heritage-based school curriculum for ages preschool up to grade seven, which promotes European culture and values, as well as teaching the history of our great [Aryan] people." Perhaps our best hope is that whoever is writing for the website also serves as a teacher, since we'll be able to identify November 9th Society members by their inability to speak or write standard English.

Anti-Racist Action activists say they're organizing a counter-demonstration for the Newark rally. One local ARA member who investigated the November 9th Society says they're a particularly repugnant and vicious strain of neo-Nazi, linked to the Outlaw Hammerskins, who in turn worship The Order, the most violent neo-Nazi organization in U.S. history.

Whether or not they take hold in Ohio may well depend on

what happens in Newark. In a press release, Newark Police Chief H. Darrel Pennington acknowledged that the November 9th Society has "extended invitations to other [white supremacist] organizations to attend." A spokesperson for the Newark Police Department says that a call for additional aid has been sent out to other law enforcement agencies.

April 12, 2001

White Noise

I had the privilege attending the March 2000 "Continuing the Journey Against Hate" conference in Chicago, sponsored by the Center for New Community. Since 1995, the faith-based Center has diligently worked with civic, community and religious leaders throughout the Midwest to combat the resurgent white supremacist movement.

Sherialyn Byrdsong—whose husband Ricky Byrdsong, the former Northwestern basketball coach, was tragically murdered in July 1999 by a neo-Nazi—was a conference organizer. So was Catherine Matthews, a doctoral fellow at Indiana, whose Korean boyfriend Won Joon Woon was killed during the same racist terrorist spree.

The specter of Byrdsong and Woon's neo-Nazi murderer, Ben Smith, hung heavy over the conference. The terrorist organization Smith served, the World Church of the Creator, were selling T-shirts in Chicago with his picture on the back proclaiming Smith "Our First Amendment Martyr." The irony—that the neo-Nazis abhor and detest the "liberal" First Amendment—easily gave way to propaganda purposes.

A new video documentary and accompanying book published by the Center, *Soundtracks to the White Revolution*, explores the questions of how a middle-class suburban youth like Smith ended up submerged in the violent white supremacist subculture.

Smith, by all accounts, entered the world of white supremacy through the "white power" music scene. Racist skinhead music helped lead him to membership in the White War Commission, a neo-Nazi gang. After his apprenticeship, he later graduated to the more ideologically established World Church of the Creator.

In the fall of 1998, Smith walked into a Chicago record store and tried to hand the store owner neo-Nazi literature. The store owner recalls this as an all-too-common event, and one he didn't think about until July 4, 1999, when he saw Smith's picture flash across CNN with his "Sabbath Breaker" tattoo now covered by longer hair.

Joining a growing phenomenon, Smith's career as a terrorist ended violently with two dead and a dozen or so wounded, before he turned his gun on himself. From his passage as jack-booted dance hall brawler and alcoholic binger to neo-Nazi hitman and martyr, Smith lived out the fantasy portrayed in white power music. In 1998, David Lane, an imprisoned member of the former neo-Nazi terrorist group The Order, proclaimed, "I am overjoyed at the success we are seeing with the white power bands... Congratulations are in order for those who are successfully using white noise."

Last summer, William Pierce, the head of the National Alliance, the most powerful neo-Nazi organization in the U.S., purchased Resistance Records, the world's largest distributor of white power music. Pierce cautiously projects that he will sell 70,000 units this year, at a $10 per unit profit margin, pumping $700,000 into his organization.

Where does all that money go? Among other activities, the National Alliance is actively leafleting in Columbus suburbs like Bexley, Dublin, Hilliard and the Ohio State University area. Pierce's objectives are straightforward, as he said in a recent National Alliance newsletter: "As Resistance Records regains strength, that acquisition should add an increasing number of younger members in the 18 to 25 age [group] to our ranks."

Resistance Records distributes bands such as The Midtown Bootboys, whose lyrics state: "Stop the threat of AIDS today/ Cripple, maim or kill a gay/ We've got to take a stand today/ We've got to wage a war on gays."

Hate Jews? Pierce has the group Mudoven for you: "You say you've seen the Holocaust/ You ain't seen nothing yet/ Six million lives will not compare/ To what you're gonna get."

Imitation One moves from the promise of genocide to specific tactics: "Slam you down into the ground you filthy slimy shit/ Break your nose and your toes and split your fucking lip."

Pierce and Resistance Records can take advantage of a network of 26 U.S. record labels and distributors that carry white power music. The bands run the gamut of genres, from heavy metal to ska to folk. Two labels are based in Ohio: 88 Enterprises in Canton and Hate Rock in Chesapeake. "88," for the uninformed, is neo-Nazi code for the eighth letter of the alphabet twice—HH, or Heil Hitler.

While George W. Bush wanders the country in a preppy frat boy stupor—running for president of the United States but unwilling to offer his opinion on the Confederate flag—he might want to check out white power albums' repeated use of the traitorous stars-and-bars battle flag of the racist Confederate South. Perhaps a quick discussion with the Confederate Hammerskins, a Southern racist gang, might set Bush straight as to what the Confederate flag stands for: The good ol' days of apartheid.

As a firm believer in the First Amendment, I'm not calling for government censorship of white power music, just increased vigilance and activism by progressives and anti-hate watch-dogs. If we wait for the mainstream media to tell us about this problem, the jackboots will already own the streets.

March 16, 2000

The Science Of Racism

Anew generation of ideologues and academicians are openly working to resurrect the most destructive and discredited ideas of Nazi science. This "new eugenics" movement must be challenged.

Eugenics is the science of improving a race stock through selective breeding and, as Nazi Germany demonstrated, has horribly frightening consequences. The search for a "master race" usually leads to genocide.

Such ideas are now slyly creeping back onto college campuses. Internationally, the Euro-American Student Unions promote campus activism on issues related to race and science. Articles posted on the group's website range from rants about "Jewish influences" to a "Call to white Americans." Most of its so-called science seems to worship the *Bell Curve* and the belief that blacks have significantly lower IQs than whites.

Ohio State University and central Ohio have a curious history relating to eugenics and Nazi scientists. As the *Wall Street Journal* wrote, "Long before cloned sheep, egg donors and sperm banks, a group of wealthy Northeastern conservatives embarked on an experiment with the help of the U.S. Army Air Corps to find a way to improve the human race... The Pioneer Fund, alarmed by the declining U.S. birthrate and rising immigration, was at the forefront of the eugenics movement."

In 1940, the Pioneer Fund agreed to pay the all-white Air

Corps members for breeding children. Two of the 12 children were Ward and Darby Warburton, twin brothers born on August 18, 1940, "at a hospital near Dayton, Ohio." Their father was stationed at a nearby airfield.

William Pierce, a former physics professor and the leader of the National Alliance, frequently refers to scientists sponsored by the Pioneer Fund in his calls for race war in the United States.

Founded in 1937, the Pioneer Fund is a nonprofit foundation with the stated purpose of studying "the problems of heredity and eugenics in the human race." Pierce's *National Vanguard* publication, citing race scientists, claimed, "It is the Negro's deficiency...which kept him in a state of savagery in his African environment and is now undermining the civilization of a racially mixed America."

Still earlier in Ohio history, the state has the distinction of hiring away H.H. Goddard from the Vineland Training School for the Feeble Minded in New Jersey in 1918. Steven J. Gould, in his *Mismeasure of Man*, called Goddard "The most unsubtle hereditarian of all...[who] used his unilinear scale of mental deficiency to identify intelligence as a single entity, and [who] assumed that everything important about it was inborn and inherited in family lines."

So impressed were Ohio public officials with Goddard's work that they hired him to head the Ohio Bureau of Juvenile Research. Sharing Ohio officials' views, according to Stefan Kuhl in his *The Nazi Connection: Eugenics, American Racism and German National Socialism*, were Nazi Party members. Kuhl points out that Goddard's pseudo-scientific writings were central to the Nazi propaganda campaign to exterminate Jews and create a master race.

Madge Thurlow Macklin, an avid supporter in the 1930s of

the controversial eugenics movement, spread the gospel of improving the human race through controlled breeding throughout North America. She co-founded the Canadian Eugenics Society in 1930, served on its executive committee between 1932-34 and acted as its director in 1935.

Macklin claimed that doctors ought to "determine who are physically and mentally qualified to be parents of the next generation." She advocated compulsory sterilization for the "unfit," like schizophrenics. In 1945, as World War II ended, she was terminated from her appointment in "medical genetics" at Ontario University.

What university would hire such a professor tied to Nazi science? In 1946, Macklin moved to Columbus and began lecturing in medical genetics at Ohio State University, where she remained until her retirement in 1959.

At the same time Macklin moved to Columbus, U.S. intelligence teams were busy rounding up Nazi scientists to bring to the U.S. to work at places like Wright Patterson Air Force Base in Dayton. This is the infamous Operation Paperclip. These Nazi scientists were most visibly linked to the U.S. space program and secretly worked on a variety of CIA projects, including mind-control experiments like the MK-Ultra project at OSU.

In 1993, a mural at the Ohio State University Medical School made international news for portraying Nazi Colonel Hubertus Strughold as one of the mural's medical heroes. In the 1960s, Strughold was painted in the mural along with other medical giants like Marie Curie and Hippocrates.

I suppose OSU officials were unaware that Strughold headed the Luftwaffe Institute for Aviation Medicine, which conducted notorious experiments on inmates at Dachau, including immersing inmates in ice water to see how long it would take them to die, forcing them to drink sea water and placing them in pressurized chambers and slowly removing the oxygen.

Nuremberg documents place Strughold at an October 1942 conference on the Dachau experiments. One scientist, Hermann Becker-Freyseng, told the War Crimes Tribunal that Strughold could have stopped the experiments at any time because he headed the institute that conducted them. The U.S. Army intelligence Central Registry of War Criminals and Security Suspects listed Strughold as "wanted."

OSU can paint over celebratory images of Nazis like Strughold, but the ideas behind eugenics can (and do) survive. As groups like the Euro-American Student Unions and Pierce's National Alliance step up recruiting efforts on college campuses and attempt to veil their hatred in academic legitimacy, we need to recognize this "science" for the racism it is.

March 30, 2000

Stand Fast
Against The Taliban

The Orwellian splendor of President George W. Bush's September 20, 2001, address to the nation struck me the next day as I encountered citizen after citizen muttering: "Bin Laden is the enemy, he's always been our enemy." With that glazed *1984* stare in their eyes, they repeated the catechism: "Either you are with us, or you are with the terrorists."

The day after the attack, even more surreal was the playing of "The Star Spangled Banner" at the changing of the guard at Buckingham Palace in England, a song written during the War of 1812 between the U.S. and Britain, the last time the continental U.S. was attacked by a foreign power.

I couldn't help but recall that when President Bush embarked on his disastrous European tour on July 11, 2001, ironically the day the U.S. government executed our own internal terrorist Timothy McVeigh, he was met by mass protests in Spain, with demonstrators bearing signs reading, "Bush, American Taliban."

Peacemakers be damned to eternal hell. The war drums are beating—the lead pipe's calling, Danny boy. We're told that we have to choose between being "with us"—the warmongers—or "with the terrorists." There's no in-between. Jesus, Buddha, Gandhi, the Pope, Mandela—back off.

We're headed into the right-wing militaristic nirvana. Endless war through "Operation Infinite Justice," where the flag-waving minions, hearts pulsing with rage and visions of vengeance demand retaliation against an ill-defined and virtually unknown enemy. But, as Gandhi put it, "An eye for an eye will only leave the world blind."

Welcome to the New Crusades. No evidence against the guilty is needed, any amorphous Third World people or religion will do. And if it all ends with the explosion of a few suitcase nukes in the United States, at least we can still cherish our very own Nuremberg Rally moment.

We should not forget that at the core of the Bush constituency are America's most self-righteous religious zealots, the Republican Taliban headed by Jerry Falwell and Pat Robertson. Within 48 hours of the terrorist attacks, Falwell and Robertson took the airwaves to use the tragedy to try to turn the U.S. in the Taliban's religious direction.

Falwell lashed out against the forces that make the U.S. different than Afghanistan: "I really believe that the pagans, and the abortionists, and the feminists, and the gays and the lesbians who are actively trying to make that an alternative lifestyle, the ACLU, People for the American Way—all of them who have tried to secularize America—I point the finger in the their face and say, 'You helped this happen.'"

Robertson said he "Totally concurred" and added another enemy: "The top people, of course, in the court system."

Perhaps this American Taliban tag-team can begin to set up some fundamentalist Christian militias and religious courts to purge the U.S. as we head off on our jihad. The face of fundamental religious fanaticism is universal.

That's why the CIA, like the Bush family in domestic politics, utilized their most fanatical and zealous religious allies, in this case the pan-Islamic extremists, in their covert operation to drive the pro-Soviet regime out of Afghanistan in the 1980s. As the axiom goes, "the United States trains the best terrorists in the world."

Bin Laden—once part of the U.S.-funded Mujaheddin—broke with the CIA in the aftermath of the Gulf War, when we saw fit, in our long-standing desire to make the world safe for cheap Gulf oil, to place a U.S. military base on Saudi Arabian soil. While it's difficult for most Americans to understand why this would enrage the Arab and Islamic world, perhaps they might ponder how we would feel if say, one of our Gulf War allies like Syria, placed a military base in the middle of the United States?

The bin Laden terrorist network carried out similar acts of terrorism against the Soviet Union when their military forces occupied Afghanistan. When the Soviet forces retreated, the bombing stopped.

To a large extent, except for Afghanistan and Iran, the Islamic extremists have been held in check throughout the Arab world. They constitute significant political forces in Pakistan, Algeria, Egypt and Saudi Arabia. If secular pro-U.S. regimes in the region are toppled as a result of the United States' continued presence and military actions there—allowing the forces of fundamentalism to come to power over more numerous mainstream Islamic believers—Bush may ultimately prove to be the Taliban's best ally.

The relationship between this extremist terrorist network and mainstream Islam is akin to McVeigh's so-called "Christian Identity" neo-Nazi ideology and mainstream Christianity. When McVeigh, in a vicious act of terrorism, blew up the federal building in Oklahoma City, we did not declare war on the Aryan Nation in Idaho or on William Pierce's National Alliance in West Virginia or the Michigan Militia that harbored and nurtured our American-born terrorist. Rather, the Republicans invited the militia movements to the Capitol so they could explain their views.

Also, why haven't we declared war against America's longest standing terrorist network—the Ku Klux Klan? Indeed, Senator Trent Lott and Representative Robert Barr, two white supremacist sympathizers, are key parts of the Bush political coalition. The African-American community may be less than enthusiastic about supporting this worldwide crusade when they're still fighting for voting rights in Florida.

There were many marginalized progressive voices that warned for two decades of the misguided and short-sighted policy of funding Islamic extremists. On May 21, 2001, the Bush administration gave the Taliban $43 million for their support of the U.S. "War on Drugs." There was no reported quid pro quo that the misogynous regime would quit oppressing women or blowing up historically significant architecture like the giant Buddha stone statues they'd recently demolished.

It's impossible to say that the United States wasn't warned and warned repeatedly regarding our relationship with the bin Laden network and the implications of our one-sided support of the right-wing militaristic Sharon government in Israel. His government has destroyed any hopes of immediate peace and polarized the region into militarist and religious extremists.

In fact, the former chief of CIA counter-terrorism operations, Vincent Cannistraro, wrote in the *Washington Post* that the Israeli policy of assassinating its enemies "is neither effective nor moral." Cannistraro pointed out that the "assassination of Abu Ali Mustafa was accomplished with American-provided helicopters and missiles—enough rationale for some terrorist group to target American citizens."

Writing just a little more than a week prior to the terrorist attacks of September 11, Cannistraro warned, "And of course it provides more incentive in state support for Osama bin Laden's operations in carrying out new violence against America. Bin Laden, far from being placed in a 'box' by the United States, has recently been successful in consolidating his position with the Taliban inside Afghanistan. Indeed, we may well see a resumption of terrorist activity directed against the United States by surrogates of the state sponsors of terrorism we had all believed to have been banished from the 21st century."

The propagandistic sloganeering brought to us Big Brother-fashion in support of "Operation Infinite Justice," which is code for Operation Permanent Warfare, is so blatantly manipulative it's laughable. How President Bush can keep a straight face when he tells us that America was targeted "because we embrace freedom" and not because of our government's actual policies in the Middle East is utterly amazing. Of course, the vast majority of Americans have rallied to the righteous jihad, perhaps better named Operation Jethro Bodine or Operation Gomer Pyle or Operation Zombie Ribbon Wearers.

Howard Zinn put it best when he said: "The images on television horrified and sickened me. Then our political leaders came on television, and I was horrified and sickened again. They spoke of retaliation, of vengeance, of punishment... Will we now bomb Afghanistan, and inevitably kill innocent people, because it is the nature of bombing to be indiscriminate?... And only now can we begin to know what people have gone through, often as a result of our policies. We need to decide that we will not go to war, whatever reason is conjured up by the politicians or the media, because war in our time is always indiscriminate, a war against innocents, a war against children. War is terrorism, magnified a hundred times."

I think of Zinn's words when I encounter the Big Brother Bush sycophants. The *Dawn of the Dead* high-fashion mall crowd who caved in immediately to the blue light special on war. There's only one thing being sold on cable TV which functions as one big advertising network and shopping channel—war.

The terrorists need to be brought to justice and tried before an international court. No doubt during that trial they will raise the issue of the 700,000 dead Iraqi children as a result of the U.S. attack on Iraq and subsequent embargo. Nothing can justify the terrorist attacks of September 11—and nothing will ever justify the death of 700,000 innocent Iraqi children.

We need to condemn *all* violations of human rights, whether it's bin Laden terrorism or a U.S. military intervention or CIA covert operations or Taliban oppression or the insane religious rhetoric of U.S. fundamentalists Robertson and Falwell.

Columbus Free Press
Autumn 2001

About The Author

Bob Fitrakis is a political science professor at Columbus State Community College, where he won the Distinguished Teaching Award in 1991. He is the author of *The Idea of Democratic Socialism in America and the Decline of the Socialist Party* (Garland Publishers, 1993) and a frequent speaker on political, labor and social policy issues at national academic and political conferences. He earned his Ph.D. in Political Science from Wayne State University and his J.D. from Ohio State University Law School.

As a columnist and investigative reporter for the weekly alternative newspaper *Columbus Alive* from 1996 to 2002, Fitrakis won 10 editorial awards from local, state and national journalism associations. "Uncovering River Valley Schools' Atomic Secrets" (page 110), co-written with reporter Jamie Pietras, won the first-place award for Best Coverage of the Environment from the Ohio Society of Professional Journalists in 2001. In 2000, "Spook Air" (page 46) won second-place prizes for Best Investigative Reporting from both the Ohio Society of Professional Journalists and the Press Club of Cleveland.

Fitrakis is the executive director of the Columbus Institute for Contemporary Journalism and has published the *Columbus Free Press* since 1992 and acted as the journal's editor since 1993. Fitrakis has co-hosted a news/public affairs program on public access television and he hosts a weekly call-in talk radio program on WVKO AM.

He was a member of the Human Rights Party in Michigan, a founding member of the Michigan Democratic Socialists Caucus, a founding member of the Democratic Socialists of America and the Democratic Socialists of Central Ohio, and he served on the National Political Committee of DSA. In March 1994, Fitrakis served as an international observer for the national elections in El Salvador and, in 1993, he visited Reynosa and Matamoros, Mexico, as part of a human rights delegation to investigate conditions in the maquilladoras.

Fitrakis was a candidate for U.S. Congress in 1992 and for the Columbus School Board in 1995. He was a ward representative on the Franklin County Democratic Party Central Committee from 1996-2000. He served on the Africentric School Advisory Board for the Columbus Public Schools and worked with the West High School College Preparation Program. He currently serves on the city of Columbus' Near East Area Commission. In 2003, Fitrakis is running for a seat on Columbus City Council as a Green Party candidate.

Printed in the United States
71711LV00001B/1-45